Beyond the Courtroom
Alternatives for Resolving Press Disputes

BEYOND THE COURTROOM

Alternatives for Resolving Press Disputes

WITH AN INTRODUCTION BY
Reese Cleghorn

EDITED BY
Richard T. Kaplar

Media in Society Series
the media institute
Washington, D.C.

Beyond the Courtroom: Alternatives for Resolving Press Disputes
Copyright © 1991 The Media Institute

All rights reserved. No part of this publication may be reproduced or transmitted in any form without permission in writing from the publisher.

First printing January 1991.

Published by The Media Institute, Washington, D.C.

Printed in the United States of America.

ISBN: 0-937790-44-3

Library of Congress Catalog Card Number: 90-63732

Table of Contents

Profiles of the Contributors		vii
Preface		xi
Introduction: Journalists in Conflict		1
Reese Cleghorn		
I.	The National News Council Is Not a Dead Issue	15
	Louise W. Hermanson	
II.	Beyond Conflict Resolution to Community Values: The State News Council and the Ombudsman	43
	Richard P. Cunningham	
III.	A Proposal for Libel Law Reform	65
	Richard M. Schmidt, Jr.	
IV.	The Libel Dispute Resolution Program: A Way To Resolve Disputes Out of Court	83
	John Soloski and Roselle L. Wissler	
V.	Alternative Routes to Conflict Resolution: Is This Trip Necessary?	113
	David Bartlett	
VI.	The British Press Council Experience	127
	Kenneth Morgan	
Index		149

Profiles of the Contributors

Reese Cleghorn is professor and dean of the College of Journalism of the University of Maryland at College Park and president of *Washington Journalism Review*, published by the school. Before academic life, he was a journalist for three decades. He was associate editor of the *Detroit Free Press*, editor of the editorial pages of the *Charlotte Observer*, an editor and reporter with the *Atlanta Journal* and the Associated Press, and editor and co-publisher of the weekly *California Courier*. He was president of the National Conference of Editorial Writers in 1980. He is co-author, with Pat Watters, of *Climbing Jacob's Ladder*, a book about the civil rights movement and the South, and has been a contributor to numerous anthologies and national magazines. He holds a Master's degree in public law and government from Columbia University and a bachelor's degree in journalism from Emory University.

Louise W. Hermanson is an assistant professor of communication at the University of South Alabama in Mobile where she teaches media ethics and law. She developed and headed a new mass communication program at Fort Valley (Ga.) State College from 1983 to 1990, and won numerous awards for writing, editing, and photography while she was a weekly newspaper editor in the early 1980s. Currently her major research interest centers on finding a workable alternative to the courts for disputes between the public and media.

Richard P. Cunningham is director of graduate studies in the New York University Department of Journalism. He has focused on press ethics and accountability since 1972 when he was appointed the first reader's representative at the *Minneapolis Tribune*. He worked at the *Tribune* for 25 years and before that was managing editor of the *Durango (Colo.) Herald News*. His first newspaper job was at the *Hartford Courant*. He was an associate director of the National News Council from 1981 until its demise in 1984.

Richard M. Schmidt, Jr. is a partner in the Washington, D.C., law firm of Cohn and Marks, specializing in communications law. A member of the Colorado and D.C. bars, Mr. Schmidt has served as general counsel of the American Society of Newspaper Editors, and Washington counsel for The Association of American Publishers, Inc. since 1969. He has lectured on communications law at the University of Denver College of Law and at Catholic University School of Law in Washington, D.C. He is a member of the Board of Trustees of the Washington Journalism Center. Mr. Schmidt received the First Amendment Award of the Society of Professional Journalists/Sigma Delti Chi in 1980, and was elected a Fellow of SPJ/SDX in 1981.

John Soloski is head of graduate studies and an associate professor of journalism and mass communication in the School of Journalism and Mass Communication at the University of Iowa at Iowa City. **Roselle L. Wissler** is research director of the Iowa Libel Research Project. Both Drs. Soloski and Wissler are members of the Dispute Resolution Program of the Iowa Libel Research Project. The other members of the program are Randall P. Bezanson, dean of the School of Law at Washington and Lee University; Gilbert Cranberg, George H. Gallup professor of journalism and mass communication in the

School of Journalism and Mass Communication at the University of Iowa; and Brian Murchison, associate professor of law in the School of Law at Washington and Lee University.

David Bartlett is president of the Radio-Television News Directors Association in Washington, D.C. He has served as vice president of news and programming for the NBC Radio Networks, managing editor of Metromedia Television News, director of news and English broadcasts for the Voice of America, and news director of WRC Radio in Washington. He began his career as a reporter for the *Hartford Courant* and has written and produced television documentaries and special programs for PBS, Turner Broadcasting, and WRC-TV in Washington.

Kenneth Morgan, OBE, is director of Great Britain's newly created Press Complaints Commission. He was director of Britain's Press Council between 1980 and its demise in 1990, after serving as its conciliator and deputy director. He had been a consultative member of the London-based council since 1970. A former general secretary of the National Union of Journalists, he has been a counselor of the Bureau of the International Federation of Journalists and is a frequent speaker for the International Press Institute. Mr. Morgan entered journalism in the north of England 40 years ago and has worked for newspapers and news agencies in Manchester, London, and Cairo. He is one of the four independent trustees of Reuters, and a fellow of the Royal Society of Arts.

Richard T. Kaplar has written, edited, or produced over 30 books and monographs on a variety of communications topics. The most recent book he authored is *Prime Time for Repeal: The Financial Interest and Syndication Rules*. Mr. Kaplar is vice president of The Media Institute in Washington, D.C. He holds a Master's degree in public administration from the American University in Washington.

Preface

The goal of this book is simple: to set forth in one place a description of the various programs, proposals, and ideas that address the ever-vexing problem of resolving press conflicts.

This endeavor has turned up a range of options that is promising if not wide. Discussions can be found in these chapters, for example, on the use of ombudsmen; the experiences and efficacy of news councils (National, Minnesota, and British); a proposal for libel law reform; and an arbitration program. While diverse, all of these have one thing in common: They are alternatives to the burdensome judicial model of complaint resolution occasioned by current libel law.

It was in that decade of excess, the 1980s, that courtrooms in New York and Washington saw several highly celebrated libel cases played out on an epic scale—*Westmoreland v. CBS, Inc.*, *Tavoulareas v. Washington Post Co.*, *Sharon v. Time, Inc.* Perhaps the current interest in alternatives was heightened by the realization that these cases could easily devour millions of dollars and thousands of hours and still not produce decisions that were always clear cut or totally satisfactory to at least someone. Cases like these hardly represent a productive use of capital—nor do they hold out much hope to the aggrieved citizen (or media outlet) of more modest means.

Therefore attention turns to finding cheaper and quicker methods of resolving complaints and restoring reputations. But, as Reese Cleghorn notes in his introduction, not everyone (and especially not everyone on the media side) believes this is a necessary pursuit. Thus this book, while trying to accomplish a simple task, finds itself stumbling into a complex web of conflicting values, at the center of which is the fundamental tension between journalists and those who would hold them accountable to some standard of conduct. American society is built on Judeo-Christian principles of normative behavior, of right and wrong. From this springs our system of laws, and the concept of the individual's accountability to the law. Contrast this to the First Amendment, a libertarian concept that places accountability for speaking out within the individual, and seeks to isolate the individual's speech from government and the normative influence of its laws.

It is no wonder that disputes are hard to settle (or that methods of resolving disputes are hard to agree on) when a complainant, typically of the normative persuasion, tries to gain redress from a journalist who believes fervently in his right to be left alone. Perhaps the real task at hand is not finding the most "workable" method of resolving disputes, but addressing the underlying conflict of values that makes the dispute-resolution question so intractable. That, however, is beyond the scope of this book.

The reader should be aware of two developments, one potential and one actual, that are discussed in these pages. The first, noted by Louise Hermanson in Chapter 1, is that the Minnesota News Council is entertaining the idea of becoming national in scope—in effect a successor to the National News Council. Its expansion would depend on obtaining funding; its success as a national body would depend on a host of other factors that Prof. Hermanson explores.

The second development is both imminent and onerous. As this book was going to press, Kenneth Morgan reported that Britain's Press Council, in operation since 1953, was indeed about to fold. (When he wrote Chapter 6 this was just a possibility, albeit a strong one.) In January 1991 the Press Council is to be replaced by a "Press

Complaints Commission," a nominally voluntary group that will labor under the threat of being succeeded by a government-controlled commission or tribunal. Could it happen here? Doubtful, although opponents of news councils are bound to point to this as an example of what can happen if advocates of "responsible" journalism have their way.

At bottom, the British experience reiterates the importance of our First Amendment in keeping government out of the journalism business. Still, conflicts will arise and will demand resolution. Given the burdensome nature of libel actions (which many people, and especially many non-journalists, view as disenchanting) alternatives for resolving press disputes must be found beyond the courtroom.

Richard T. Kaplar, Editor
Washington, D.C.
December 1990

Introduction: Journalists in Conflict
Reese Cleghorn

In the end there may be no better way to settle a conflict between an editor and a reader, or between a broadcast journalist and someone in the news, than the old-fashioned way: a punch in the nose, some tar and feathers, a bullet in the leg, or more equitably, pistols at 20 paces. A book that deals with peaceable ways to settle conflicts between press and public, or press and public officials, presupposes that these conflicts should be settled, and settled in a civilized manner. Not everyone would agree with that.

Some would argue that any quasi-official or official body that formally judges the press (print or broadcast) must establish criteria, which amount to standards; and so even if there is no penalty for the judgment, journalists have been shown a leash. Unless they want to be considered pariahs, they accept the leash. More and more precedents are established. Soon these might as well be codified. Behold! We have an established code of conduct. If it is prevalent, we have something close to licensing.

This kind of reasoning may be dismissed as hysterical or paranoiac. After all, even the American press already is under many external controls. It is subject to penalties for libel, violation of copyrights, and certain invasions of privacy; and there is a body of statutes and legal precedents related to all this that might be considered a code or a set of standards. The press is also subject to taxes, health and occupational safety regulations, and a variety of other legal and regulatory constraints that apply to industry, and it has a vested interest in postal rates. The government has exempted parts of the press from antitrust legislation in certain circumstances, and the government decides when the exemption may apply. And, of course, a major part of the press—broadcast journalism—has always been bound by the regulation of the broadcast industry.

Therefore it might seem that any absolutist interpretation of the First Amendment ("Congress shall make no law respecting an establishment of religion, or prohibiting the free exercise thereof; or abridging the freedom of speech, or of the press....") has long since been compromised. But, in fact, the First Amendment has withstood seeming contradictions without being vitiated. It retains its vitality and its essence, whether related to religion, speech, or the press. It is germane and central to any serious discussion of the press and judgments of its performance, even if the remedies being discussed (independent news councils, for instance) are constitutionally acceptable.

The First Amendment was so fundamentally radical and audacious that two centuries later it still confounds and even exasperates many people. They are unable to accept it without thinking there must be more to it. The First Amendment is vexatious because it speaks not only to government, warding off interference, but also to the press, inviting it by implication to be defiant and even obnoxious in exercising its unique role in American society. What the amendment does not say is at least as important as what it does say. It says nothing, of course, about a "responsible" press (or "responsible" free speech or "responsible" religion), and there is nothing in it or surrounding it that suggests the press would have to be responsible in order to keep its freedom. Thus, ardent First Amendment advocates in the press may well resist any kind of mechanism that calls for quasi-judicial review of the press's performance: not because it is a violation of the First Amendment's protection against government regulation, but because it rests upon an asssumption that the press must be responsible. Advocates also believe review mechanisms violate the spirit of the First Amendment by imposing another kind of societal control that has the same effect.

In sharp contrast to this libertarian (or classical liberal) point of view, the concept of responsibility and accountability is the bedrock of the British government's recent efforts to curb the press, as recounted in Kenneth Morgan's chapter in this book. In most of the world, the British government's position would seem reasonable and, given the putrid nature of much of the British press, justifiable. Let this be a useful reminder of how peculiar the American approach really is. In an American context, the British government's warnings to the press would be outrageous: perhaps popular in some quarters, but clearly an assault not just upon the press but upon the First Amendment itself and its entire evolution in judicature.

Beyond the Courtroom: Alternatives for Resolving Press Disputes explores, chapter by chapter, several approaches to resolving conflicts between the press and the public: news councils to consider complaints against the press; media ombudsmen who investigate complaints; mediation and arbitration mechanisms dealing with legal questions. The authors are not all singing from the same songbook. In fact, it seems evident that they would not agree on some of the most basic issues.

Kenneth Morgan, director of Great Britain's new Press Complaints Commission and former director of the British Press Council, obviously believes in the council's work and is pleased to note that it had been a model for councils in other nations. He describes the origins of the council and explains how it worked. His commitment to self-regulation in the press is complemented by the conviction that an official government commission to oversee the British press is a "chilling thought."

Louise Hermanson, a doctoral candidate at the University of Minnesota, writes about the evolution of news councils and examines the work of the National News Council (1973-1984). She advocates the creation of councils in each state and the revival of a national council. Given the history of resistance to news councils on the part of much of the press, it seems unlikely that her proposal will be accepted any time soon. But she offers some fresh ideas.

Richard M. Schmidt, Jr., a leading authority on libel who has counseled and represented newspapers and the American Society of Newspaper Editors, deals with alternatives to courtroom conflict in libel matters. He is not among those lawyers who fear losing clients if less confrontational approaches are applied in libel disputes, and he is more willing than some journalists to seek practical remedies that may not glisten with pure philosophical principles proclaimed from the ramparts. Mr. Schmidt describes the work of the Libel Reform Project of The Annenberg Washington Program. Newton N. Minow, former chairman of the Federal Communications Commission and now director of The Annenberg Program, launched the libel project. "His hypothesis was that the current libel system is not working well for anyone," the project's report says. "It neither adequately protects First Amendment values nor provides plaintiffs with an effective way to vindicate their damaged reputations." The project proposed a Libel Reform Act "to provide an efficient and speedy remedy for defamation, emphasizing the compelling public interest in the dissemination of truth in the marketplace." Mr. Schmidt explains the proposed legislation and presents arguments for and against it.

Another approach to resolving libel disputes is outlined by John Soloski, head of graduate studies in journalism and mass communication at the University of Iowa, and Roselle L. Wissler, a fellow member of the Dispute Resolution Program of the Iowa Libel Research Project. The program's experimental work began in 1987. It has examined the motivations of plaintiffs who have sued the media, concluding that they are primarily concerned with the question of truth or falsity in the alleged libelous material and with restoring their reputations, rather than with monetary compensation. If that be so, and if the press's response is based upon its sense that a libel suit is as much an assault upon its integrity as an effort to rob its cash register, there are more efficacious and reasonable ways to resolve libel conflicts than costly courtroom battles (in which, ultimately, the forces with the most money have the upper hand). Would the Iowa solution create, by establishing a body of precedent, what amounts to a national set of standards? It might very well do that, but this already is being accomplished inadvertently in libel and privacy decisions in the courts, where expert witnesses often are called upon to measure a news organization's performance against "accepted professional standards." (This is a sleeper that journalists and others should be watching more closely.)

David Bartlett, president of the Radio-Television News Directors Association, offers a skeptical view of these and other proposals for resolving libel conflicts. He doubts that any of these proposals "would significantly improve on the system already in place, imperfect as it is."

"The American media are not responsible to the government," he concludes. "Journalists will always remain outsiders, accountable only to their readers, listeners, and viewers."

Another dimension to the discussion is provided by Richard Cunningham, director of graduate journalism studies at New York University. He also writes about instruments for resolving conflicts but looks beyond them to raise questions about the nature of ethical analysis of the press's work. "Journalists today do not speak in a language that is adequate for this dialogue," he writes. "They answer complaints in a shop talk that is incomprehensible to readers and viewers. The appropriate language for creative dialogue between press and public is the language of ethics."

Ombudsmen and news councils, Professor Cunningham argues, should use ethics language (rooted in the philosophical study of ethics rather than in the conventional wisdom of journalists). This, in turn, might encourage journalists "to use ethical analysis to make editorial decisions." It is not quite clear how this would work out, and I suspect that it might not be as he wishes. He looks at a case in which the *Hartford Courant* exposed racial bias among real estate people by sending out reporters pretending to be prospective clients. The paper's disclosures of bias were laudable, he believes, but were outweighed on the ethical scale by the fact that reporters were dishonest about their identities.

This seems to be an easy call for Professor Cunningham. He writes that "it doesn't take a Ph.D. in ethics to make such judgments." Maybe not, but was the judgment the best that could be made within a framework of ethical analysis? Many journalists defend the use of false identification in certain situations, contending that it would be unethical to fail to use an approach involving subterfuge to expose a dangerous poison such as housing discrimination. A journalist holding that view may hedge it this way: The subterfuge is excusable if a story important to the public may not be obtained by other means.

Not all but many cases of conflict between the press and individuals entail subjective judgments about what is "ethical" or "professional" or "standard practice." Thus it is impossible to consider mechanisms for resolving conflicts without also considering the basis on which these judgments, essentially value judgments, are to be made. Even if they are made on an ad hoc basis case by case, a body of precedent emerges and it thereafter may become the measure of what is "ethical," "professional," or "standard practice." When considering the approach advocated by Professor Cunningham, journalists may fear the imposition of rules made by people who do not share their understanding of their role. Perhaps oversimplifying, they foresee a set of prohibitions without a corresponding set of mandates for accomplishing their work; or perhaps they fear the latter as much as the former. Among the prohibitions, for instance, might be these:

- Journalists should never deceive anyone about their identities.
- Journalists should not stealthily "stake out" someone's house, thereby invading that person's privacy, in order to obtain information.
- Journalists should not use unnamed sources, or should not do so unless the information is separately corroborated by one or two independent sources.
- Journalists should publish no accusations unless they have enabled the accused to offer a rebuttal.
- Journalists should set themselves apart from their communities by not joining any organizations that may be the subject of their reporting or that may have advocacy roles on public issues.

"Standard practice" on these matters varies from one situation to another, and from one publication to another. In attempting to codify and qualify any of these prohibitions, as some news organizations do, we immediately run into a tangled web of subjective judgments. Are they to be based upon accepted general practice among journalists, and if so is there an accepted general practice on any of these questions? If they are to be grounded in a philosophical discipline called "ethics," how? Does that grounding provide answers to the questions raised here, or does it simply offer a framework within which to think about the question? If it is the latter, will not journalists come to one conclusion while philosophers come to another?

Defining the journalist's role is central in all this. When journalists see themselves as defenders of the commonweal and watchdogs of the public trust, they may be more inclined to rationalize practices—occasional deceit about their identities, for example—that would not be accepted by someone who believes journalists have no right to act as self-appointed scourges of wrongdoing. Further, refraining from publishing or broadcasting certain information may be at least as unethical as publishing information that damages individuals for no good reason. The ethical code of the Society of Professional Journalists includes a mandate "to serve the truth," which may override some lesser considerations.[1] If a newspaper fails to report or interpret certain trends and developments in its area that are important to the public, perhaps not because of any collusion or deliberate protectiveness but because of being sluggish, unaggressive, or unwilling to disturb its readers, would that be called unethical? Shouldn't it be? These quandaries are not likely to be resolved by the creation of explicit standards to be applied to all. So is it a good thing to establish news councils or other tribunals, whether or not they are dominated by members of the press, to make judgments about press performance? The answer may depend upon how restrained such a council may be, and upon how widely its judgments are accepted as standards for the press to follow; in this formulation, restraint may be a virtue but wide acceptance of the standards may be malign, leaving too little room for parts of the press or individual journalists to speak freely.

In this country, one of the most important documents dealing with the improvement of journalistic practice came from the 1947 report of the Commission on Freedom of the Press, known as the Hutchins Commission.[2] Its work still provides a great intellectual framework for examining the role of the press in a democratic society. The commission was headed by Robert Maynard Hutchins, chancellor of the University of Chicago. Its 13 members included such important thinkers as Reinhold Niebuhr, the theologian; Arthur M. Schlesinger, the historian; Harold D. Lasswell, Yale law professor and one of the founders of communication research and studies of propaganda; Archibald MacLeish, poet and one-time State Department official; and Zechariah Chafee Jr., Harvard law professor. The commission had the financial support of the Encyclopaedia Britannica and of Henry R. Luce, the head of Time, Inc. One might have thought that this combination of intellectual and financial power would have a great and immediate impact. It did not. The press reacted to the report by attacking or ignoring it.

The most negative response was to this proposal: "We recommend the establishment of a new and independent agency to appraise and report annually upon the performance of the press." The commission said this agency, "independent of government and of the press" and supported by gifts, should broadly examine press performance, help establish standards, investigate sins of commission and omission, and seek wide publicity and public discussion of press issues.[3] Other parts of the report have been largely forgotten. It is especially important to note the core of the commission's position: "We do not believe that the fundamental problems of the press will be solved by more laws or by governmental action."[4] It did suggest changes in law and regulation, but the changes were intended to expand rather than restrict freedom of the press (for instance, by extending constitutional guarantees to radio). Its recommendation of "centers of investigation, graduate study, and critical publication" in communications is fulfilled today by a diversity of schools of journalism and mass communication, as well as by centers studying press performance, that did not exist or existed only in modest form in 1947.

In the 1940s the American press rarely reported on itself in a significant way. The commission responded to this silence: "We recommend that the members of the press engage in vigorous mutual criticism. Professional standards are not likely to be achieved as long as the mistakes and errors, the frauds and crimes, committed by units of the press are passed over in silence by other members of the profession.... The formal organization of the press into a profession, with power in the organization to deprive an erring member of his livelihood, is unlikely and perhaps undesirable. We have repeatedly evidenced our desire that the power of government should not be invoked to punish the aberrations of the press. If the press is to be accountable—and it must be if it is to remain free—its members must discipline one another by the only means they have available, namely, public criticism."[5]

Whether the "vigorous mutual criticism" suggested by the commission is available today depends upon where you sit. The work of ombudsmen is described herein by Professor Cunningham. The movement has taken hold at a limited number of newspapers, but despite some exceptionally good performances, most of these in-house reader representatives have not provided the depth and breadth of critical analysis that had been envisioned by the original enthusiasts. On the hopeful side, some news organizations have shed their traditional reluctance to report on the press. Major newspapers now have media critics, some of them excellent. Television occasionally produces a worthwhile review of press performance. But most Americans do not regularly read or see substantive work in this field, and there are limits to the range and firepower of most in-house critics.

In scholarly work, the amount of useful analysis is proliferating, some of it significantly expanding the parameters of the discussion. Unfortunately, even the best of this work usually escapes the notice of journalists in the field. Among journalists, the principal independent analyses of press performance are found in two national journalism reviews, both established long after the Hutchins Commission's report: *Columbia Journalism Review (CJR)*, founded in 1961 and published by the Graduate School of Journalism of Columbia University, and *Washington Journalism Review (WJR)*, founded in 1977 and now published by the College of Journalism of the University of Maryland. Both have national circulations of about 30,000. Some other national publications publish analyses of press performance but are not primarily journalism reviews. (Honest disclosure: As dean of the college at Maryland and president of *WJR*, I have a vested interest in journalism reviews.)

Journalism reviews should, and I believe often do, offer the kind of "vigorous mutual criticism" within the press that was advocated by the Hutchins Commission. They themselves are journalism, not academic journals. Nor are they quasi-judicial in nature with reports based upon a council or committee's deliberations of fact, followed by conclusions. Thus they do not conjure fears that an accumulation of their articles may come to constitute a body of approved standards applicable to all journalists or to those of a particular place in the media. In fact, their most valuable contribution may be in presenting a diversity of thought about issues in the practice of journalism. Both publish reports, reviews, commentary, and letters by journalists and non-journalists, often with opposing views.

Novelist Larry McMurtry, who was then a member of *WJR's* advisory board, addressed the question of whether the review should formulate a set of standards or create professional debates when he wrote in the first issue: "The value of any journalism review seems to me to depend largely upon the kind of questions it chooses to ask.... Does news do any harm, does it do any good, is it really an agent of culture or merely one of the innumerable idle pastimes with which we distract ourselves? Such questions may be hard to answer, but surely the first business of a journalism review should be to register them."[6] In a pilot issue of *CJR*, the editors said the review's goals would include these: "To deal forthrightly with what it finds to be deficient or irresponsible and to salute what it finds to be responsible, fair, and professional. To discuss all the means that carry news to the public, thus viewing the field whole, without the customary partitions. To provide a meeting ground for thoughtful discussion of journalism, both by its practitioners and by observers, to encourage debate, and to provide ample space for dissent."[7]

The impact of the reviews is difficult to measure, but market research has shown that *WJR* and *CJR* are read closely by thousands of reporters, editors, publishers, and broadcast managers. These readers are aware, when they make tough decisions about content, that someone will be looking over their shoulders, with no power to punish except the "public criticism" urged by the Hutchins Commission. Judging from responses in the form of rebuttal articles and letters to the editor, the sting of criticism that is read by colleagues in the field can be extremely uncomfortable. *WJR* has cited these words from the Washington bureau chief of a major national newspaper: "The final test is: How will it look in the *Washington Journalism Review?*"

The two national reviews were established in decades when there was a sudden burst of energy in media criticism. Besides the establishment of news councils and ombudsmen's offices, the 1960s and 1970s produced local journalism reviews in many major American cities. All of these have disappeared except for the *St. Louis Journalism Review*. The local reviews had an insufficient economic base for survival after the first months or years of dedicated work by highly motivated editors and writers. Another factor may have been that some reviews sprang to life because of perceived abuses and failures by local and regional news media and became a part of a journalistic counterculture, or at least represented an anti-establishment impulse: a "revolt of the slaves," said journalist James Aronson.[8] A magazine of general circulation, *Saturday Review*, called the *Chicago Journalism Review* "a strident, controversial compendium of political sniping, gutter language, encomiums to local favorites and cronies in press and government, Chicago chauvinism, rasping hostility toward the boss, seamy exposes, and occasionally, incisive reports."[9]

For the most part, the analyses and reports in *WJR* and *CJR*, vigorous as they often are, fall far short of the expectations of the scholars and other critics who challenge the basic premise that the content of the press must remain free of regulation by government (or, in the case of broadcast journalism, must become free of it) and also free of formal codes and standards established by the prevailing forces in journalism. Has the American press become such a powerful institution, allied with dominant economic forces and increasingly owned by giant media companies and conglomerates, that it now limits rather than expands freedom of speech? If so, is the First Amendment's guarantee of freedom of speech separable from its guarantee of freedom of the press?[10] To answer these questions in the affirmative, one must see the press primarily in corporate and institutional form: an impersonal colossus, rather than the complex joining of media corporations and professional impulses. My faculty colleague Carl Sessions Stepp advocates a "professional responsibility model" as the best defense against any kind of content regulation on the one hand and press abuses on the other. He argues that we should strengthen the professional impulses that exist in newsrooms, so that journalists increasingly see themselves as "independent, accountable professionals," with less porous walls between them and their corporate hierarchies.[11]

American journalism is, in fact, both a business and a profession, unless one defines a profession as a field in which the practitioners are bound by established, mandatory codes and perhaps also licensed by the state. Journalists live in a professional limbo: responsive to the influences, values, and judgments of their colleagues and to a kind of professional ethos, but without fixed rules for admission to or expulsion from their calling. They are right where the First Amendment left them: in the only commercial enterprise that is specifically protected in the Constitution and Bill of Rights. Perhaps they should forever hang there, uncomfortably suspended between the respectability of professions such as law and medicine that abide by formal self-regulation, and the rogue status of unruly artisans.

Notes

[1] *Code of Ethics* [Adopted in 1926 and revised in 1973, 1984, and 1987], (Greencastle, Ind.: Society of Professional Journalists), para. 1. The *Code of Ethics* may be obtained from the society at 16 South Jackson St., Greencastle, Indiana 46135.

[2] Leigh, Robert D., ed., *A Free and Responsible Press, Report of the Commission on Freedom of the Press*, (Chicago: University of Chicago Press, 1947).

[3] *Ibid.*, pp. 100-102.

[4] *Ibid.*, p. 80.

[5] *Ibid.*, p. 94.

[6] McMurtry, Larry, "News without end, amen," *Washington Journalism Review*, premiere issue, Oct. 1977, p. 5.

[7] "Why a review of journalism?" [Unsigned one-page statement by the editors], *Columbia Journalism Review*, pilot issue, Fall 1961. Reprinted in *CJR*, Vol. I, No. 1, Spring 1962, p. 2.

[8] Aronson, James, *The Press and the Cold War*, (Indianapolis: Bobbs-Merrill, 1970), p. 286. For calling this comment to my attention and for other background on some of the reviews, I am indebted to Dennis, Everette E. and Rivers, William L., *Other Voices: The New Journalism in America*, (San Francisco: Canfield Press, and London: Harper and Row, 1974).

[9] Cited in Dennis and Rivers, *supra*, pp. 83-84.

[10] This view is developed by Judith Lichtenberg in "Foundations and limits of freedom of the press," in Lichtenberg, Judith, ed., *Democracy and the Mass Media*, (Cambridge, England: Cambridge University Press, 1990), pp. 102-135.

[11] *See* Carl Sessions Stepp in *Democracy and the Mass Media, supra*, pp. 197-199.

I. The National News Council Is Not a Dead Issue

Louise W. Hermanson

A number of groups have tried to force social responsibility on American media, and one method has been through news or press councils. The Minnesota News Council, begun in 1971 and serving only the state of Minnesota, is the one remaining adjudicative council in the country.[1] The National News Council, the only other American news council to adjudicate cases, was begun in 1973 and died in 1984. These two councils have been the best known and most successful in calling the media to task for ethical violations, but their only power rests in publicity of decisions. Their impact on media performance has been questionable.

The concept of news councils dates back to the 1870s in Sweden. The best known council is the British Press Council, begun in 1953. In the United States, the push for an evaluative news council has existed since 1947 when the Hutchins Commission called for media to accept the responsibilities of common carriers and for the public to establish an "independent agency to appraise and report annually upon the performance of the press."[2] The Hutchins Commission's study warned that if the American media are to remain free, they must be more responsible; encouraging discussion of newsgathering practices and answering to an independent evaluative body was seen as part of that responsibility. The concept is based on an understanding of checks and balances. Since the media criticize all other aspects of American society, the independent agency would, in turn, serve as a check on media power by criticizing irresponsible media performance. The concept of an evaluative body lay dormant for a number of years and was revived during the late 1960s and early 1970s, a time of heavy media criticism by public figures and politicians.

Other types of news councils have existed in various localities throughout the country since the early 1950s, but they are mainly discussion groups where media executives invite prominent members of the public to comment on how a medium covers the community. These councils include bodies like the Editorial Page Advisory Board and the Editorial Advisory Board of the *Macon (Ga.) Telegraph and News*. The two advisory boards are each made up of 15 to 20 members of the community who meet periodically, but not regularly, at the invitation of the newspaper's managing editor or editorial page editor to discuss coverage, critique columns, and consider balance in the pages of the paper. Public members of the boards are chosen by the newspaper's management from the "more substantial people in the community," said Ed Corson, editorial page editor for the paper. But "sometimes people sort of invite themselves by being obnoxious."[3] Results of the meetings are not made public and most readers are not aware of the groups' makeup or meetings, although periodically the paper will run information about the boards. Corson said the paper uses the boards to obtain feedback from the public since there is no independent news council in the middle-Georgia area.

Because media organizations instigate the discussion councils, they are designed to fit news media purposes. As with the Macon groups, most meet in private, frequently at a local restaurant, to discuss coverage of the community, and there is no attempt to enforce, or even suggest, a formal ethical standard regarding the media. There are no formal decisions concerning right or wrong, and almost no publicity about the discussions appears. The value of each council is dependent on the integrity of the media organization's management, which uses the meetings to explain newsgathering to influential members of the public and to expand the medium's base of contacts for story ideas. The purpose of the discussion councils is educational rather than judicial.

The National News Council's Purpose

In 1971, shortly before the Minnesota News Council adjudicated its first case, the Twentieth Century Fund established a special task force to "examine the feasibility of establishing a press council—or councils—in the United States."[4] In 1973, as a direct outgrowth of the task force's study, the National News Council began operation as an adjudicating council. The express purposes were strikingly similar to those of the 1947 Hutchins Commission's call for an independent agency to report on press performance,[5] although the Twentieth Century Fund report almost ignored the Hutchins Commission and specifically said the body it was proposing was modeled after the British and Minnesota councils.[6]

The National News Council's charter addressed almost all of the Hutchins Commission recommendations, including the goal of serving as an outlet for the good of society. It said the purposes for which the corporation was formed were charitable, educational, and scientific. The National News Council was begun as a private and independent institution to:

- serve the public interest in preserving freedom of communication and advancing accurate, fair reporting of news;
- affirm the values of freedom of expression in a democratic society;
- promote public understanding of those values and the responsibility of the public as well as the media for their preservation;
- initiate research and issue reports on these matters;
- provide an open and independent forum to receive, investigate, and report on complaints involving the accuracy and fairness of news reports disseminated by the nation's major print and electronic media;

- consider complaints from members of the media concerning the conduct of individuals and organizations toward the nation's major print and electronic media;
- review and report on attempts to restrict access to information of public interest; and
- make public its findings.[7]

Periodically, the National News Council published reports of its activities, including a listing of all decisions on complaints heard by the council. The National News Council lived ten and one-half years before the advisory board voted to end its operation, mainly, many speculate, because of difficulty in obtaining funding.[8]

The National News Council faced many of the problems encountered by other news councils of all types, such as lack of funding, no tested formal structure, and media arrogance. But the National News Council also had to address problems associated with the large number of news organizations and the complex regional diversity of the country. The founders decided it would be impossible to handle complaints from all citizens about all media organizations throughout the country. For these reasons, the National News Council was restricted to hearing complaints and studying issues of national importance involving national media, such as newspapers with national circulation and impact, news magazines, broadcasting networks, and news services.

The National News Council tackled abuses on a variety of national issues in spite of a lack of support from many national news suppliers, such as the *New York Times*. As with the Minnesota News Council and the legal system, the vast majority of complaints were withdrawn, settled, or died for lack of action. Even when the council found against a medium, the only power was in the publicity the council could generate for the decision. It could not fine media found to be in violation of journalistic standards or force any type of apology or restitution.

In 1983, the National News Council received contributions from 6 foundations, 38 media organizations, 21 corporations, and 13 individuals.[9] These results came after repeated fundraising efforts by news council staff with specific appeals tailored to the four aforementioned groups.[10] It is revealing that more than 1,500 individuals contacted the National News Council for help with problems with the media, but fewer than 100 individuals contributed to funding of the council. Eight of the individuals who contributed in 1983 were on the National News Council or its advisory board, and this pattern of support changed little throughout the life of the council.

In addition to hearing complaints from the public, National News Council staff published position papers concerning free press/fair trial, press-police cooperation in covering crimes, use of unidentified sources, and an evaluation of editing practices after Janet Cooke's "Jimmy's World,"[11] a case in which a fabricated story was published as a feature in the *Washington Post*. But the council was more than decisions and reports. In a letter from Norman Isaacs, then National News Council chairman, to Michael J. O'Neill of the *New York Daily News*, Isaacs talks of the "lightning rod function" as only one function of the council:

> The bulk of our work never shows in any public record. ...Yesterday alone, for example, we were (1) seeking to explain journalistic accountability — and its limits—to Dr. Michael DeBakey; (2) culling the files for a raft of material on terrorism and the media for Peter Straus, who is taking on two study projects...on the subject; (3) opening a discussion with Ben Bradlee about his views of the balances needed in reporting on cancer exploration...; studying a (com)plaint from Milwaukee that coverage of the missile-sites debate was unbalanced...; and submitting to a telephone interview by a graduate student at Northwestern...about the ethics involved in reporters who do the old posing-as-somebody else to do their investigative reporting.... Last week we all spent part of one day sitting with the *Kansas City Star & Times'* new ombudsman to give him all the information we had about how the job seems to work best, the major problems, on and on....[12]

In spite of its successes, the National News Council was not able to obtain adequate funding or to gain the respect of important national news suppliers. In addition, few members of the public knew about the council. The majority of complainants to the council were from the major metropolitan areas of Washington, New York, and California, and the council was accused of being elitist in selection of its members. Although the concept was said to be sound, the council voted to cease operation shortly after its 10-year evaluation. Hostility from media organizations played a major role in its death.

A Question of Revival

In 1987, the Minnesota News Council began receiving complaints from citizens of other states about media in their areas. As of March 1990 the council had received 33 out-of-state complaints,[13] although it had accepted none of the complaints for adjudication. But this out-of-state interest, bolstered by General William Westmoreland's statements that he would have used a news council if one had been available when he brought his lawsuit against CBS in 1985, caused supporters of the national news council idea to see the Minnesota News Council as the most likely group to succeed on the national level. They argue that the Minnesota News Council's 20-year history of adjudicating cases on the state level can provide the experience necessary to solve problems associated with the national body. Funding proposals have gone to several foundations, and eager Minnesotans, such as Otto Silha, a long-time supporter of the Minnesota News Council, feel the Minnesota Council has the experience to make a success of another national council.[14]

Whether supporters of a revised adjudicating national news council are successful in their attempts will hinge on careful balancing of the three purposes of an adjudicating news council. Evaluation of problems that existed with the National News Council is imperative, and creative solutions to gaining and maintaining public and media respect and support must be found. The original National News Council expressed a clear understanding of the three-pronged function of a council: (1) to give the public a forum for complaints about media performance; (2) to give the media feedback concerning how the public perceives their role in a democratic society; and (3) to give society unbiased reports on how the media respond to responsibilities individual members of a democratic society have to the whole. These three functions involve three distinctly different elements: the media, the individual complainants, and members of society who have a vested interest in maintaining freedom of the press. The National News Council had problems in all three areas and with all three groups. It was only partially successful in gaining acceptance from the media, convincing the public the council was unbiased, securing adequate funding, and providing for adequate publicity for the council's work.

A Forum for Complaints

A greater long-term goal of a news council is to help provide a system for individual citizens to complain effectively about media performance. This system must somehow balance power between the media and individuals as well as the free speech and free press clauses of the First Amendment. It should also provide a way for someone who has been harmed by a news medium to bring the injustice to the attention of the medium's audience.

The National News Council claimed to be a dispute-resolution system for average citizens who had complaints about American news media performance. The concept included accepting for adjudication complaints without valid legal claims as well as providing an alternative to the courts in libel and invasion-of-privacy suits. National News Council staff touted the council as a viable means for the average citizen to fight back against irresponsible media. The opening narrative of the National News Council report published in 1984 carried this statement:

> "You *can* fight City Hall. Even when it's a newspaper," the headline said over an article in the July 1980 issue of the magazine *medical economics*. The subtitle read: "When this doctor's fees were erroneously inflated in a news story, his demands for retraction were ignored. But a watchdog agency got him even more."[15]

The narrative went on to explain that the doctor's complaint was an example of what the council could do for citizens wronged by the media, and pointed out that the council not only found for the doctor, but the newspaper ran a front-page story on the decision. The doctor is quoted as saying: "Being, by nature, somewhat cynical, I was surprised to get anything near this much redress of injustice. It shows that if you're right—and willing—you can fight 'bad press'—and even win."[16] The doctor had indeed gotten a decision in his favor and vindication in the pages of the newspaper that had harmed him. It is possible the doctor could have won a libel suit against the medium if he had chosen the courts instead of the council. But the remedy he received was as good or better than any that could have been awarded by a court. It also involved much less time and expense than bringing suit.

The remedy provided by the council in the doctor's case fits well into the concept that defamation is best remedied by giving those originally exposed to the defamatory statement corrected information. Efforts to provide this type of remedy have long existed in state retraction statutes, which give protection from significant damage claims to publishers willing to print a correction or retraction after they publish erroneous information.[17] The idea of publicity as the best way to correct wrongs has persisted in scholarly writings as a sane, sensible way to resolve disputes with the media since early American retraction laws were passed in the mid-1800s. A recent non-governmental effort to convince the legal profession that correction is the best remedy in defamation was the Annenberg libel reform proposal which said "the simplest, most efficient remedy for defamation is a prompt and reasonable retraction and reply."[18]

The National News Council claimed to serve as a true alternative to the legal system and took steps to assure that the news council would be used as an exclusive remedy rather than just another phase in the legal arena's discovery process. The National News Council published this note in its instructions about how to complain to the council:

> Those complaining to the Council are required to sign a waiver stipulating that no legal action is under way or

contemplated. The reason for this is that the Council is an alternative form of settling disputes—totally apart from courts or administrative bodies such as the Federal Communications Commission. As such, it is not willing to have its research or findings used in legal or government actions.[19]

J. Edward Gerald, a noted supporter of the news council concept, said the legal waiver is an important element in the process. "Grievants are advised of this (legal waiver) policy at the outset and can make a free choice. They are not deprived of a right to tell their story by choosing to go to court (instead of the council). The difference in costs is, however, one strong recommendation for choosing to take disputes to the council."[20] Emphasis on choosing a council because it is cheap indicates that a council can provide a poor man's forum for justice, a valid and noble pursuit.

The National News Council logged 1,253 complaints between 1973 and 1984. It took no action of any kind on 199, dismissed 827 without formal hearing, and gave full hearing culminating in the issuance of determinations in 227.[21] It found against the media at least partially in 77 of the complaints. The full council actually heard and decided fewer than 19 percent of the complaints received and found against the media fully or partially in only 82 of the 227 decisions, an overall warranted rate of less than 7 percent.[22] In the early years, the council seldom found against the media, with only 16 complaints out of 100 upheld in the first three years. In later years, more decisions were against the media, with 27 of 43 upheld during the last three years. Some speculate that the council became more selective in the cases it would accept for adjudication in the later years as it became more experienced in handling complaints.

According to council records, most of the complaints were dismissed because they did not conform to council guidelines for dealing with complaints, were not within the scope of the council's established area of attention, or complainants decided not to pursue the matter. A closer look at the files shows that complaints that were clearly articulated received much more attention than those that were emotional, contained fragmented thoughts, or were written in non-standard

English. Many complainants who did not articulate their complaints well were sent polite letters which said that the matter simply was not within the council's purview. Staff spent little effort investigating such complaints.

The Nature of Complaints

Much has been written about the media's response to the news council process, and much of this response has been negative. Many media representatives have gone on record as viewing the news council process as just another form of harrassment, and they are reluctant to support a process that produces self-inflicted wounds. Several major articles have appeared in law journals about how a news council can solve some of the problems faced by plaintiffs who take on powerful media in legal disputes, and the social value of news councils has been discussed by United States Supreme Court justices in at least two decisions.[23]

But the third element in the news council process has largely been ignored. An adjudicating news council provides a service to the individual members of society who feel wronged by the more powerful media. The council gives individuals an opportunity to speak in a forum with impact, and it provides an opportunity for vindication. Therefore the reactions of individuals who complained to the council is vital to an understanding of the usefulness of news councils in our society.

Very little is known about who complains to a news council or what they hope to accomplish by such actions. Until recently, no one had asked complainants what they thought about the news council process or whether they thought the process was worth their time. Only two studies were found that addressed the process from the complainants' perspective and both focused on the Minnesota News Council. The studies were very limited in scope, using a very small number of respondents, and each focused on media satisfaction with the process, using complainants' surveys as incidental to the study. Robert Schafer's thesis focused on how the media responded to the Minnesota News Council, but he also surveyed 38 complainants to determine if they thought the council was biased and whether they approved of the council. On a five-point scale ranging from biased to not biased, the average was 2.53, not a resoundingly favorable rating. Complainants did report they were pleased with the news council process, although about a fourth of them found the procedure time consuming and confusing.[24] Fred Johnson's 1975 study of the Minnesota News Council included only 24 usable responses. It showed complainants overwhelmingly supported the council but did not feel performance of the media had improved because of its existence.[25] No studies were found to address how National News Council complainants viewed the process or the overall value of the news council process.

In 1989, a study of those who complained to the National News Council was undertaken by the author of this essay. The study focused on complainants who saw their cases through to determination since these cases represent issues important enough for the council to agree to schedule them for hearing, and they involve complainants who were interested enough to follow through. Although addresses in the National News Council files were up to 16 years old and a number of complainants could not be found, 70 complainants representing 73 of the National News Council decisions responded to the survey. They reported information about themselves, what they had hoped to accomplish by complaining to the news council, and how they valued the process. Information about complainants can be found later in this essay.

Complaints to the National News Council ranged from vague carping about the media in general, to third-party complaints where the person felt someone else had been wronged, to carefully formulated, well-thought-out expressions about specific events involving the complainant. Examples of complaints that did not go to hearing include a complaint that the news media "destroy the reputation of many innocent men and women." The complainant gave no specific examples and made no direct references concerning a situation which should be addressed directly. Another complainant wrote to the council requesting help because the media would not cover the National Nudist Council's efforts to put its members in political offices. He provided no information concerning media outlets he had contacted or targeted for his coverage. The council dismissed the complaint as one which could not be processed given the rules set up by the council for handling disputes involving the media.

Of the complaints heard by the full council, most were presented to the council in carefully articulated, well-thought-out letters of complaint, regardless of whether they were complaints from first or third parties. That these should receive more attention is not surprising, since specific complaints following all the rules are less time consuming to handle and usually indicate that the person will follow through if additional information is needed. A person who has made the effort to understand the system and work within the specified guidelines already has an investment in the process.

The council received formal, written complaints from a variety of people of varying sophistication. Some came from legal professionals who understood there was no legal-system solution for many media-related ethical problems, and the complaints were presented with the precision of those highly skilled in dealing with disputes. An example is the third-party complaint made by a person who worked within the criminal justice system in Hawaii. She complained because *Parade* Magazine, in a story titled "How To Win a Free Trip," unnecessarily published the name of a rape victim. The story was about Hawaii's practice of paying full expenses for the return of victims to the islands to testify in trials against their assailants. The complaint came after the complainant had contacted the magazine, and she included a copy of the letter from *Parade* with her original complaint. Council staff began an investigation and contacted *Parade*. The case was dismissed without a hearing by the full council after representatives from the magazine agreed to reasonable actions concerning future incidents involving similar circumstances.[26] The National News Council files indicate the council would probably have heard and decided on the case if it had not been resolved between the complainant and *Parade*.

Some well-presented cases were not heard because the complainant did not wish to conform to council rules. One complainant sent a six-page letter outlining the specifics of her complaint about an article in *New York* Magazine titled "The Nightmare Comes True: A Victim's

Story." She carefully spelled out what she perceived to be a violation of her off-the-record agreement with the writer and clearly detailed the problems she encountered because the specifics of her experience as a mugging victim were published in a feature story. The case appeared to have serious merit, but the complainant requested anonymity, something the council could not grant based on the rules of procedure. The case was dismissed.[27]

Although most complainants were on their own in articulating complaints, there is some indication that the news council tried to help complainants formulate their problems into acceptable formats. One example is the letter from Charles Mendelson complaining about the publication of the name of a 14-year-old rape victim, an issue eventually included in the council's larger investigation for a position paper concerning publication of the names of rape victims. The letter of complaint received by the council was handwritten and vague about the problem, but Executive Director William Arthur and the news council staff, recognizing the seriousness of the complaint, requested additional information from Mendelson and others involved until enough information was received to warrant bringing the issue before the full council.[28]

Another example of the council's attempts to formulate a complaint from one received in incomplete format involved a letter to the council from a man who stated that he did not know the proper procedure for making a complaint. The complainant raised the question of whether a newspaper should be allowed to keep morgue clippings containing inaccurate information. The incident the complainant referred to happened more than 20 years before, and the council had a policy requiring that cases be filed within 90 days following the conduct, action, or publication of the material complained about. However, the policy allowed discretion for the council's executive director, and William Arthur saw potential for addressing the morgue issue. A half-inch-thick file containing correspondence, clippings, etc., beginning July 1, 1976, and ending April 26, 1977, contains several three- to four-page letters from the complainant trying to provide additional information so the council could address the problem. The case was finally dropped "because of the time lapse."[29]

Several problems with the National News Council system made articulating complaints to the council difficult. First, many persons simply did not know the council existed as an alternative to the legal system or as an outlet for valid complaints about media ethics. Moreover, because no laws addressed such concerns, complaints involving ethics had no standing in the legal framework.

Second, frequently the 90-days-after-publication rule did not give adequate time for a complainant to go through the process of working through his complaint, deciding the council could help him, and producing the complaint in articulated form. For example, the complainant was required by the council to try to work out the dispute with the news organization before a complaint was filed. Then, when the complaint was filed with the council, the complainant was required to sign a waiver stipulating that no legal action was underway or contemplated. A complainant who thought he might have a legal claim would be reluctant to sign such a waiver until he had gone to an attorney and found that the claim had no legal merit, was not covered by the legal system, or would be too costly or time-consuming to litigate. Such a claim against journalistic practices may have merit in the interest of freedom of the press, and an arbitration system such as the National News Council may be the only outlet for such a complaint. However, by the time the complainant worked through the problem to accept this and articulate the complaint in proper form, more than 90 days could easily have passed.

Third, the council's "How to Complain to the National News Council" was designed to state the process simply and encourage contributions, but it failed to include some of the rules for arbitration.[30] In addition, the terminology used by the council in referring to disputes, especially in the early years of the council's operation, looked and sounded much like that of the legal system, leading some potential complainants to assume the procedure would also be complex.[31] The frustration factor can become significant if the complainant must work to understand the system, learn additional rules, provide additional information, and become heavily involved in the process. At any point, the person may simply decide pursuing the matter is too much trouble and opt out.

A User Profile

An analysis of cases decided by the National News Council reveals the council dealt with a number of cases that could have been taken to the courts, and the survey of complainants who pursued their cases to the determination stage shows that complainants were anything but poor or uneducated.[32] These facts indicate that news councils can indeed serve as an alternative to the courts, and the fact that they have not stems from media opposition, lack of publicity, and lack of availability rather than from deficiencies in the structure and procedures of the councils.

The average National News Council respondent in the 1989 complainants' survey was a white male born before 1933 who had at least a Master's degree and a household income of more than $50,000. Forty-nine percent reported household incomes of more than $75,000, and only 3.6 percent reported incomes of less than $25,000. Twenty-seven percent had doctoral degrees, and only 12 percent were not at least college graduates. Almost 40 percent were Republican, with the remainder split almost equally between Democratic and Independent political philosophies. Forty-eight percent were active politically. Sixty-four percent were representing individuals in their complaints to the news council and another 33 percent were representing organizations, social causes, businesses, or governmental bodies. These statistics indicate that the National News Council served an elite population rather than serving as a forum for the average person.

Survey respondents overwhelmingly chose newspapers as the best source for news. When asked to select among newspapers, magazines, television, and radio, 54 percent selected newspapers as the preferred source on conflicting reports, and more than 80 percent selected newspapers for local news. Fifty percent preferred newspapers for national and international news. Respondents reported that the media basically do a good job but they feel reporters' values frequently influence stories and reporters often mislead the public. Respondents reported they value a free press even if it is irresponsible.

It has long been argued that a major purpose of news councils is to educate the public about the newsgathering process. Respondents, however, do not agree. Although respondents overall think the existence of a news council makes the press more responsive, more than 60 percent reported their involvement with the council did not increase their understanding of how news organizations operate or make decisions.

Sixty-four percent of the respondents rated the news council concept valuable and almost 23 percent more rated the concept useful, but they were less favorable when they evaluated the decision in their particular case. Forty-two percent said news councils are better than courts for solving disputes with the media, and 57 percent said there would have been no one to complain to about their case if there had not been a news council. Although respondents reported a variety of dissatisfactions with the news council process and decisions, 50 percent said they would use a news council again if they had a dispute with a media organization and one were available. Fifty-seven percent said they think the media are too powerful for the average person to win against in any forum, but they reported that they felt they at least had to try. More than half of the respondents thought the news council process was fair.

A number of respondents expressed appreciation for the chance to be heard, and they reported that they wanted vindication of their positions against the more powerful media organizations. They saw the news council as an opportunity to express their frustrations, but many said they were offended because they were not allowed to participate actively in the process. Some felt the council was biased, and almost all felt the council should have included more average citizens and fewer media representatives and professional superstars.

One respondent said: "Too many of the media's representatives have this 'greater than God' attitude in the face of challenge to their work and their decisions. They aren't *always* right; there is usually more than *one* way to do the job well. A little more humility and less outright defensiveness would help the public's image of the media. I'll fight, as most Americans will, to keep our freedom of the press, but the press, having been granted almost unbridled freedom, must find better ways to demonstrate the responsibility that goes with such freedom—freedom that most professions and other occupations don't have."

Another expressed the frustration of an individual who has no formal system through which to fight the media now that the news council has ceased to function. "The situation is frustrating! We are in the position of the flea biting the dinosaur: We draw no blood. We are completely ineffective. The influence this dinosaur wields is frightening. Our forefathers were not prophets. They could not foresee the technology that would create the awesome power of the press, a power that intimidates the people and dwarfs our government."

Another respondent said: "Some kind of counterbalance of the media is needed. I won my National News Council judgment, and my attorney said I might have won a libel judgment against *Time*, but the cost would have been hundreds of thousands of dollars and might have dragged on for years. The individual is no match for Time, Inc., with its millions and millions in resources. I feel they were morally and ethically bound to print a retraction or an apology or summary of the National News Council finding. In any future council, the power to enforce publication should be built in."

Another respondent explained why his involvement with the council was frustrating: "The fact that our leading publications did not honor the decisions of the council sort of made it simply an effort to get personal satisfaction. The *New York Times*, the *Washington Post*, and many of our major publications did not accept, or take part in the work of the council. It sort of reminds me of the World Court in Geneva, where the United States chose in advance not to accept the decision concerning the mining of the harbors in Nicaragua. Since no one has the power to make a publication accept a decision, and since most of the media in New York ignored the decision (were they worried that it might be them next time?), the decision was only a personal victory, and not more than 25 people know about it."

Concerning the need for another council, another respondent said: "Letters to the editor are not enough. When the media mislead—intentionally or not—they need to be taken to task, held accountable. A news council is one form of accountability. The media hold public officials/organizations/etc. accountable through their stories all the time. To be fair, the media should agree to be similarly exposed by printing an article when they are found 'guilty' by the news council."

Overall the survey data indicate respondents are very well-educated, affluent individuals who do not hate the media, although they see a number of negative sides to newsgathering and reporting processes. Respondents see freedom of the press as an important societal goal, and they think news councils can contribute to that goal. Frustration about the system becomes apparent in their responses to questions about where individuals can complain about media sins and how much effect those complaints have on the long-term practices of the media.

The National News Council was criticized for its elite makeup of highly placed, influential persons throughout the country. It appears from the 1989 survey that the council also served an elite constituency of complainants with high educational and income levels. More study is needed to determine whether average Americans did not complain to the council or whether they were weeded out through the news council's operating procedures.

Conclusions

The news council concept is a good one. A news council can provide a forum for citizens to be heard and can provide vindication when the media harm members of society. A willingness to accept criticism could go a long way toward enhancing the image of American media. But a national news council is not enough. In addition to a national news council, there should be a council in each state, with well-trained arbiters who hear complaints about media performance. In Minnesota, the newspaper association took the lead in developing a council, and the associations in other states would do well to follow the lead.

Written determinations stand as the official decisions of a news council. Although there has been talk about using National and Minnesota News Council decisions as precedent for future cases concerning media ethics, the idea has received opposition from a number of directions. Refusal to use these decisions as precedent means any council must decide all complaints on an *ad hoc* basis, and no carefully analyzed foundation for making decisions in the newsroom is built. News council decisions could provide information to journalists throughout the country about how their peers solve ethical problems, and they could let the public know that journalists are indeed concerned about credibility.

Phil Duff, editor of the *Red Wing (Minn.) Republican Eagle*, a charter member of the Minnesota News Council, and a member of the Minnesota Newspaper Association board when that council was formed, said he saw the council idea as a way to hear from press critics without trespassing on the First Amendment. Publishing information about the council helps increase the credibility of his paper, he said:

> [I]n dealing with newspaper people who are kind of alarmed about the council on a theoretical basis, I respond, "Why should we be?" If the press council does make a finding against you and you publish a story about it in your newspaper, as you are obligated to do, what's so terrible about that? If you still think you are right, write your editorial and say you are right. It is no worse than having somebody write a critical letter which you publish. You live with that—that's not the end of the world—and then you go on.[33]

Another Minnesota News Council charter member, Jerry Ringhofer, editor of the *Owatonna (Minn.) People's Press*, said:

> If you can stand to have someone look over your shoulder, if you can afford or allow the public to have a "tribunal of last resort" without going to court, that's a strength, not a weakness. I have felt that if you are doing your job right you don't have to worry about who is looking over your shoulder.... If we are doing the best we can, I don't know why we should fear accountability....
>
> It bothers me at times when the Associated Press carries a notation in its press council stories that the organization has no power. I think the council's power of publicity is a potent weapon.[34]

News councils can realistically serve as alternatives to the courts. Many persons who bring lawsuits want vindication, and a news council is uniquely qualified to provide that type of remedy. It addresses disputes with the media in their language, and it expects them to give publicity to the decisions. A court does not do this. There is no obligation, moral or other, to publish information about a lawsuit against an information medium. Using more informal adjudicatory processes, a news council can fulfill the goals of alternative dispute resolution systems, such as mediation and arbitration, found to be useful in other areas of the law.

But to limit a news council to serving as an alternative to the courts is unwise and impractical. A news council should not be limited to hearing only cases involving legal questions. Its greatest strength is in the capabilities of its members to analyze ethical issues as well.

For news councils to succeed, several things must be accomplished:

- The media must be convinced to support and cooperate with the council.
- Adequate publicity must make the public aware such a system exists.
- The public must be convinced to trust the news council to be fair.
- The news council must provide services to all levels of society, not just to public figures and the elite.
- The news council must be adequately and independently funded.
- News councils must gain the respect of the legal profession and convince lawyers and judges to recommend their services.
- There must be no perception that news councils provide second-rate justice to those who have no place else to go.
- News councils must provide ways for complainants to participate actively in hearings.
- A national news council should exist to hear complaints about national media, and a state council should exist in each state so that councils can become an accepted part of the media/public equation.

Media need some incentive to support councils. As they are structured now, councils merely provide another social institution the newspaper or broadcasting station has to deal with. If news councils can indeed become a viable alternative to libel suits and this can be demonstrated, media should be eager to participate, suffering a little of the inconvenience for relief from high damage awards. This also should reduce libel insurance rates.

One of the problems with news councils is that they must depend on the media for publicity. If the media do not want to support a council, no one knows it exists. Even in areas where news councils have functioned most successfully, few members of the public have been aware of them. Journalists themselves are unaware of attempts to start news councils in their own areas. A November 1989 survey of 65 state media-organization leaders in 46 states revealed that only 12 of the respondents were aware of any discussion or attempt to start a news council in their state. Twenty-eight of the respondents said they simply did not know if an attempt had been made to start a council in their state. Only one respondent asked for more information.[35]

Creative ways to help the public become aware of news councils abound. On a March 1989 episode of "L.A. Law,"[36] a focus group of scientifically selected "jurors" was used to facilitate settlement in a liability suit against a pharmaceutical firm. Hypothetical researchers carefully picked focus-group members to simulate an average jury, and the "jurors" heard scripted arguments in the case. The purpose was to determine how a jury would react if the case were to go to trial. The pharmaceutical firm wanted to evaluate its chances of winning, and when it saw that a jury would probably empathize with the plaintiffs, top management decided to settle. Through this episode, viewers were introduced to a real-life alternative dispute-resolution system used in more progressive areas of the country.

A 1980 episode of "Lou Grant" could have just as easily, credibly, and entertainingly brought the "*Tribune*" before a news council. Consistent with the theme of the show, it could have addressed a serious ethical/legal dilemma, such as libel or invasion of privacy. Through this story line, a viable alternative method of solving disputes with the media could have been publicized throughout the country. But no such show aired. If news councils are to exist in the future, they must devise ways to make their existence known to the public.

If news councils are to establish public and media trust, council members should be trained in arbitration and ethical reasoning so that they approach cases in systematic fashion. It is not enough to be willing to do the job. Properly trained council members could provide arbitration in binding and non-binding decisions, and judges and lawyers could divert cases to the panel in cases that now have no place to go but the courts, even if the main goal of the plaintiff is vindication. A national pool of news council arbitrators could be used throughout the country and travel to a specific geographic area to hear cases, thus providing complainants more opportunity to participate in the hearing process.

Arbiters should have training in journalism, law, or ethics, and the best place for selecting persons with appropriate backgrounds would be colleges and universities. They could be nominated by organizations such as the Association for Education in Journalism and Mass Communication, Society of Professional Journalists, American Bar Association, and the American Arbitration Association.

Parties to the dispute would select three arbiters, one selected exclusively by each and the third agreed upon by the parties. Selection would be made based on qualification profiles prepared by the national news council. Parties using the council as an alternative to the courts could contract as to whether the decision was to be binding, but each contract would include an agreement that the medium concerned would run the decision, regardless of who won. If appeal rights were retained and the appealing party did not better his position by certain standard, preset criteria, he would be liable for legal costs for both parties.

Once trained, arbiters would remain in the pool as long as they desired or until they were asked to resign. There should be no exclusion of a well-qualified, highly trained arbiter because of length of time on the panel. Arbiters should be paid expenses and a reasonable amount for the time involved. To do this, the news councils must find steady, reliable sources of funding from groups or organizations that will not dictate policy.

With this type of system, state media organizations could lobby legislatures for retraction laws that would limit or prohibit damages in a case where the media outlet ran the news council decision. This would be a tangible incentive for media to cooperate with news councils.

As the Minnesota News Council looks at the possibility of going national, it must address a number of practical problems. Some way to handle cases from varied geographic areas must be worked out so that complainants can participate in the hearings, so they will feel they are an important part of the process. A system that overlooks this important need of complainants is sure to have many of the problems the National News Council faced. Modern technology provides possible solutions. Such things as teleconferencing during the hearings and using satellite technology to transmit news council hearings across the country could enhance the image of a national news council.

Members of the public are going to criticize media conduct regardless of whether journalists cooperate. Journalists can gain from involving themselves in the discussions instead of finding out about the lack of support through loss of readership, moves for controls on the press, or the filing of lawsuits.

It is time to rethink the way we approach freedom of the press, and to be creative in finding solutions to some legitimate complaints about media performance. News councils can provide a way for the media and the public to participate in preservation of freedom of expression. It is time to convince both sides that news councils can work for the good of society without infringing on First Amendment freedoms of the press or the public. They can provide a forum for intelligent discussion of issues related to continued media freedom, and encourage a diversity of voices about what the media should provide for society.

The goal of the First Amendment is to provide protection for all speakers, not just those who own the presses. News councils can provide a forum for all to speak about the ideas presented by the nation's most influential and powerful communicators, and they can serve to balance the power for those who feel powerless when faced by the professional communicators who run the media. Media should have nothing to fear from encouraging a diversity of voices and opinions about what they do. They should welcome the feedback in a nonpunitive forum that helps them understand the public they serve, and encourages citizens to learn more about how journalists do their jobs.

Notes

1. For information about the history of news councils see Chapter 3 of "News councils as alternative dispute resolution," an unpublished Ph.D. thesis by Louise W. Hermanson, University of Minnesota, 1990. Additional information about unsuccessful attempts to start adjudicating councils is found in the unpublished "Report of the first meeting of the Task Force to Study the Feasibility of Establishing a News Council in Wisconsin," and "Minority Report," Madison, Wis., Feb. 24, 1981. Copies of these reports are in the J. Edward Gerald files in the Silha Center for the Study of Media Ethics and Law, University of Minnesota, Minneapolis, Minn.

2. Leigh, Robert D., ed., *A Free and Responsible Press, Report of the Commission on Freedom of the Press*, (Chicago: University of Chicago Press, 1947).

3. Telephone interview, Jan. 12, 1990.

4. *A Free and Responsive Press*, (New York: The Twentieth Century Fund, 1973), p. v.

5. McKay, Robert B., "National News Council as national ombudsman," *Saint Louis University Law Journal*, Vol. 21, 1977, pp. 102-112.

6. *A Free and Responsive Press*, *supra* note 4, pp. 5-6.

7. Certificate of Incorporation, National News Council, Inc., National News Council Archives, Social History Welfare Archives, University of Minnesota, Minneapolis, Minn.

8. "The news council—what did it in?" [Editorial], *Columbia Journalism Review*, Vol. 23, No. 1, May-June 1984, p. 25.

9. *In the Public Interest—III*, (New York: National News Council, 1983), pp. 564-566.

10. National News Council Archives, Social History Welfare Archives, University of Minnesota, Minneapolis, Minn.

11. *In the Public Interest—III*, *supra* note 9.

12. Norman E. Isaacs, Chairman, National News Council, to Michael J. O'Neill, Jan. 21, 1982, original in National News Council Archives, *supra* note 10.

13. Pam Fanning, Administrator of the Minnesota News Council, Minneapolis, Minn., to Louise W. Hermanson, March 5, 1990, original in hand of author.

[14] Otto A. Silha, President, Silha Associates, Minneapolis, Minn., to Charles L. Overby, Gannett Foundation, Washington, D.C., Jan. 17, 1990, photocopy in hand of author.

[15] *In the Public Interest—III*, supra note 9.

[16] *Ibid.*, p. 2.

[17] Sanford, Bruce W., *Libel and Privacy: The Prevention and Defense of Litigation*, (New York: Harcourt Brace Jovanovich, 1985), pp. 479-82; Fleming, John G., "Retraction and reply: Alternative remedies for defamation," *University of British Columbia Law Review*, Vol. 12, 1975, pp. 15-31; "Recent cases: Libel and slander—validity of statute limiting recovery in newspaper and radio defamation to special damages where correction is made," *University of Pennsylvania Law Review*, Vol. 99, 1950, pp. 107-132.

[18] *Proposal for the Reform of Libel Law: The Report of the Libel Reform Project of The Annenberg Washington Program*, (Washington: The Annenberg Washington Program in Communications Policy Studies of Northwestern University, 1988), p. 20.

[19] *In the Public Interest—III*, supra note 9, p. 580.

[20] J. Edward Gerald memo to Cam Blodgett, Administrator, Minnesota News Council, Oct. 19, 1980. In J. Edward Gerald Files, Silha Center for the Study of Media Ethics and Law, *supra* note 1.

[21] National News Council Archives, *supra* note 10.

[22] *In the Public Interest—III*, supra note 9, p. 6; and *In the Public Interest—III*, Supplement, (Minneapolis: Silha Center for the Study of Media Ethics and Law, 1983).

[23] *Miami Herald Publishing Co. v. Tornillo*, 418 U.S. 241 (1974) and *Gertz v. Robert Welch, Inc.*, 418 U.S. 323 (1974).

[24] Schafer, Robert Mills, "The Minnesota Press Council," unpublished Master's thesis, University of Minnesota, Minneapolis, Minn., 1982.

[25] Johnson, Fred, "The Minnesota Press Council: A study of its effectiveness," *Mass Communications Review*, Winter 1976-77, pp. 13-19.

[26] National News Council Archives, *supra* note 10.

[27] *Ibid.*

[28] *In the Public Interest—III*, *supra* note 9, pp. 399-404.

[29] National News Council Archives, *supra* note 10.

[30] "How to complain to the National News Council," *In the Public Interest—II*, (New York: National News Council, 1978), p. 437.

[31] Administrative records of the National News Council, National News Council Archives, *supra* note 10.

[32] Hermanson, Louise W., "News councils as alternative dispute resolution," unpublished Ph.D. thesis, University of Minnesota, Minneapolis, Minn., 1990.

[33] J. Edward Gerald interview with Philip S. Duff Jr., editor of the *Red Wing Republican Eagle*, Oct. 17, 1980, in Red Wing, Minn. Transcript in the J. Edward Gerald files at the Silha Center for the Study of Media Ethics and Law, *supra* note 1.

[34] J. Edward Gerald interview with Jerry Ringhofer, editor of the *Owatonna People's Press*, Jan. 23, 1981, in Owatonna, Minn. Transcript in the J. Edward Gerald files at the Silha Center for the Study of Media Ethics and Law, *supra* note 1.

[35] Survey conducted by Louise W. Hermanson.

[36] Aired as a repeat December 28, 1989.

II. Beyond Conflict Resolution to Community Values: The State News Council and the Ombudsman

Richard P. Cunningham

It requires looking at the glass as half full rather than half empty, but it is possible to see in the nation's one state news council and in its handful of news ombudsmen the way toward a more socially responsible press.

A state news council or a newspaper ombudsman provides an effective means for resolving journalistic conflicts. But the work of a news council or ombudsman can offer a more important good: It can go beyond conflict resolution to encourage dialogue that can define and redefine the roles of the press. If future state or regional councils and ombudsmen will take on the responsibility for creative dialogue between the press and the public, they may rescue the press from the suspicion and alienation that are now a threat to its continued freedom. And in that process, they can provide a forum for the discovery and refinement of local community values at a time when national community values seem unclear.

The goal must be to tap into that reservoir of honor among journalists that has energized every significant effort to encourage press accountability.

A state council or an ombudsman of a newspaper or broadcast news station provides a less threatening forum than a national news council (or a court) in which to discuss conflicts, to be sure. But the state council and the ombudsman also provide a forum in which to consider broader press concerns with some hope of carrying on the discussion in a framework of commonly held community standards.

Journalists today do not speak in a language that is adequate for this dialogue. They answer complaints in a shop talk that is incomprehensible to readers and viewers. The appropriate language for creative dialogue between press and public is the language of ethics. If ombudsmen and regional news councils begin to use the language of ethics to comment on conflicts that come before them, it may encourage journalists to use ethical analysis in making editorial decisions. If journalists do that, they will be better able to reply to complaints in terms that increase public understanding of and support for the journalistic process.

When we talk about journalistic honor, we are talking about the desire that is shared by a significant number of copy editors, reporters, producers, and proprietors to be proud of what they and their news organizations do for a living. That honor has been an important element in all the years of searching for effective mechanisms to encourage accountability consistent with freedom in the United States press. And those efforts go back many more years than most journalists—much less readers and viewers—realize.

Capitalizing on that honor is the most reliable way to achieve a balance of press freedom and press accountability. The best way to capitalize on that honor is through mechanisms that are both local and voluntary, *i.e.*, ombudsmen and regional or state news councils.

State News Councils

The Minnesota News Council has been and remains the only state news council permanently established to deal with complaints against the press. It consists of 24 members—12 public and 12 connected with the news media. It receives complaints, takes steps to conciliate them, and if those steps are not successful (and if the complainant is willing to waive whatever rights he or she might have to sue), the council holds an open hearing and renders a judgment on whether or not the complaint is valid. The council has no authority to subpoena or punish, and it relies on publicity about its findings as its only sanction.

The founding of the Minnesota council in 1971 illustrates the importance of the journalistic honor that we must learn to encourage. In this case the honor manifested itself among journalists on both sides of the labor-management line.[1] On one side of the line were Robert Shaw, manager of the Minnesota Newspaper Association, along with two publishers, Philip Duff of the *Red Wing (Minn.) Republican Eagle*, and Gordon Spielman, publisher of a weekly in Trimont, Minn., and chairman of the publishers ethics committee. They began talking in 1970 about establishing a grievance machinery within the publishers association to deal with complaints against member newspapers.

At the same time on the other side of the labor-management line, Bernie Shellum, a *Minneapolis Tribune* reporter active in the American Newspaper Guild, and John Carmichael, the local guild secretary, were talking about how the guild might focus on problems of journalistic ethics. The guild activity prodded the publishers lest the guild preempt the moral high ground, and they formed a Minnesota Press Council with Shellum as a member. (The name was changed to News Council later when the group extended its coverage to broadcast news organizations.)

Another element in the formation of the Minnesota News Council should be recalled when future news councils are formed. It was the input from an academician, Prof. J. Edward Gerald of the University of Minnesota School of Journalism. Gerald, whose field of scholarship was press accountability, was the expert in the United States on the makeup and function of the Press Council in Great Britain. Under his guidance the Minnesota News Council patterned itself after the British body, which had existed since 1953. It has not been common for working journalists to listen to academicians, but the Minnesota News Council experience demonstrates how shortsighted that prejudice is. Without Gerald's background and idealism, the Minnesotans would not have known how to proceed. Without the work of present-day scholars, news council members and ombudsmen would have no resource with which to measure their effectiveness.[2]

From 1971 through 1989 the Minnesota News Council received 1,240 complaints. Eighty-four went through the hearing and adjudication process. The rest were either conciliated by bringing the complainant and the appropriate editor together, or were not followed through by the complainant. The council made judgments in the areas of accuracy, confidential sources, sensationalism, privacy, polling, and questions surrounding access for opinions opposed to those of the news organization.

By dint of scrupulous care in balancing the ideal against the realities of daily and weekly journalism, the Minnesota News Council has won the cooperation of virtually all journalists in the state except Stanley Hubbard, owner of KSTP-TV. Hubbard has called the council members "vigilantes" and "busybodies" and has voiced an objection similar to that voiced by Arthur Hays Sulzberger, publisher of the *New York Times*, when the now-defunct National News Council was formed. Hubbard has said: "When you start having voluntary news councils, the next thing you might have is a government news council."[3]

The Minnesota News Council has lived from hand to mouth for 19 years, but it is respected to the point that four newspapers outside Minnesota have recommended it to their readers as a potential appeals body. The *Hartford Courant*, the *Seattle Times*, the *Riverside Press Enterprise*, and the *San Francisco Bay Guardian* have all referred disgruntled readers to it. As a result of modest publicity about those actions, by March 1990 the Minnesota News Council had received 33 complaints from outside Minnesota against out-of-state news organizations. The council was clearly tempted to "go national."

One of those complaints was against National Public Radio. It asserted that an NPR reporter should have been disqualified from reporting a story because he held book and movie rights to the story. The council's excitement about the prospect of going national was evident in a news release about the NPR complaint. The news release said: "The Council is the only U.S. media panel designed to judge journalists and news organizations for conflicts of interest, professional ethics, fairness, accuracy, and access." Whether the council should indeed take on outside complainants in a major way would depend to a large degree on the response to the council's request for major foundation funding.

The complaint against NPR brought the Minnesota News Council up against a fundamental question: Would it judge complaints against news organizations that had not accepted its jurisdiction voluntarily? NPR had not.

Michael Waller, executive editor of the *Hartford Courant* and formerly of the *Kansas City Star*, says the cooperation with a council must be voluntary. Waller, a supporter of ombudsmen and news councils, believes that the National News Council failed primarily because it did not limit its complaint handling to those news organizations that accepted its jurisdiction voluntarily. When an editor was confronted with a complaint, his reaction was: "Who appointed you guys to judge?" NPR asked the same question of the Minnesota News Council.[4]

Louise W. Hermanson, assistant professor of communication at the University of South Alabama, who studied the Minnesota and National News Councils for her Ph.D. thesis, insists that a council must be independent, meaning that it must not be governed by whether an individual news organization will cooperate. She believes that no council can survive on the few cases that would result from dealing only with willing news organizations, and she believes that the resultant lack of experience among members of a council that so limited itself would make it an incompetent hearing body.[5] (For a fuller discussion see Hermanson's essay at Chapter 1 of this book.)

But in Canada the news council movement is much stronger than in the United States. Every province except Saskatchewan has a news council, and media participation is in fact voluntary. The councils take complaints only against those newspapers that are members of the council. If the papers are not members, they agree to give the council jurisdiction in any given case.[6]

Looking at Canada can be instructive for people concerned with expanding state or regional councils in the United States. The formation of the Ontario council, for example, provides another example of journalistic honor at work. In 1972 Belend Honderich, president of TorStar, publishers of the *Toronto Star*, recruited the publishers of seven other dailies and formed a council to make their newspapers accountable to the public. As in the case of Minnesota, journalistic honor was tapped on both sides of the labor-management line. On one side were Honderich and his fellow publishers; on the labor side the Ontario publishers found an enthusiastic executive director in Fraser MacDougall, Ottawa bureau chief of the *Canadian Press*. MacDougall said in an epilogue in the Ontario Press Council's annual report when he retired in 1986: "Everything fitted in with my own feeling that the public in a free and democratic society has a fundamental right to have some say in the quality of its news reports."

Today all 43 English-language dailies and 71 community papers in Ontario are members of the press council. And while those papers are voluntary members, it would be foolish to say that their motivations to join were in every case Simon pure. The Kent Commission, a government study panel, expressed concerns about monopoly ownership and accountability in 1982. As a result a proposal was made to provide government funding for a grievance machinery to hear complaints against newspapers that were not members of effective provincial news councils. In a nation where press freedoms were not, at the time, protected by such a guarantee as our First Amendment, such a threat of government involvement was taken more seriously than it would have been in the United States; many laggard publishers joined existing provincial news councils, and provinces without councils started them.

Nevertheless, says MacDougall, the fact is that councils in Ontario, Alberta, and Quebec, as well as a community complaint council in Windsor, Ontario, were started well ahead of any threat of governmental interference, and their founders were motivated by journalistic honor.

Canadian journalists have exhibited that same honor in the establishment of another mechanism to encourage journalistic accountability: the news ombudsman. Seven of Canada's approximately 100 daily newspapers have appointed ombudsmen. If the same ratio were applied to the approximately 1,600 dailies in the United States, the number of United States ombudsmen would be over 100. As it is, there are only 32.[7]

News Ombudsmen

The news ombudsman is a newspaper employee whose job it is to represent the reader in his or her complaints against the newspaper.

In 1982 the Organization of News Ombudsmen (ONO) adopted a set of guidelines, the most important of which was: "The ombudsman must be independent, and that independence must be real. He or she should be answerable only to the person with the highest authority over the news department."

ONO said the ombudsman must "represent the reader who has complaints, suggestions, questions, or compliments; investigate all complaints and recommend corrective action when warranted; serve as an in-house critic," but "defend the newspaper publicly or privately when warranted."

The ombudsman's objectives, according to ONO, should be "to improve the fairness, accuracy, and accountability of the newspaper; to enhance its credibility; to strive to improve its quality; to make the newspaper more aware of the concerns and the issues in the community."

The first contemporary news ombudsman was John Herchenroeder, appointed at the *Louisville Courier-Journal* and its sister paper, the *Times*, in 1967 by editor Norman Isaacs. Isaacs appointed Herchenroeder eight days after he read an article in the *New York Times Magazine* by A. H. Raskin in which Raskin excoriated the press for failing to turn on itself the light of criticism it directed with such vigor at government, unions, and businesses. Raskin suggested a department of internal criticism whose head "ought to be given enough independence in the paper to serve as an ombudsman for the readers, armed with authority to get something done about valid complaints and to propose methods for more effective performance of all the paper's services to the community, particularly the patrol it keeps on the frontiers of thought and action."[8]

Several newspapers appointed ombudsmen over the next few years. They were often prompted by the experience of being out of touch with local black communities during the riots of the late 1960s and '70s. Among the newspapers that appointed ombudsmen in that early wave were the *Washington Post*, the *Minneapolis Tribune* (where, in another instance of journalistic honor, the staff requested that an ombudsman be appointed), the *St. Louis Post-Dispatch*, and the *Milwaukee Journal*.

While it is true that Herchenroeder was the first contemporary news ombudsman, it is important—for the sake of putting all such efforts into a longer historical context than is generally recognized—to note that Herchenroeder was part of a continuum of concern about accuracy and fairness going back more than 50 years. Ralph Pulitzer appointed Isaac D. White as head of what White called the Bureau of Accuracy and Fair Play at Pulitzer's *New York World* as long ago as 1913,[9] and such bureaus still exist at many newspapers. One of the duties of the first ombudsman at the *Minneapolis Tribune* in 1972, for example, was to take over that newspaper's ongoing Bureau of Accuracy and Fair Play. That meant sending clippings of news stories to people who had appeared in those stories and asking them to answer and return questionnaires on the accuracy and fairness of the reporting and the headline.

Also, in the case of Norman Isaacs, it is important historically to recognize that he did not, like Paul, experience a sudden conversion to accountability in 1967. Isaacs' commitment to accountability had its roots a generation before in the teachings of his own father, and the mentoring of an incorruptible sports editor named Eddie Ashe. Isaacs devoted time, imagination, money, and energy trying unsuccessfully to get the American Society of Newspaper Editors (ASNE) to establish a grievance committee, even going so far as to schedule an annual meeting of the ASNE in England, where the members might allay some of their anxieties by observing the workings of the British Press Council. Isaacs and his publisher, Barry Bingham, had urged community leaders in Louisville to establish a local news council.

Two things are worrisome about the attitude toward press ombudsmen today. One is the objection most editors raise to appointing more of them. The other is the misconception that the ombudsman is, or ought to be, a press critic.

Editors commonly believe that if they are doing their job right, they are functioning as ombudsmen. More than half of the editors responded that way in a survey by graduate student Kent Lauer at Oklahoma State University in 1989. (Another 26 percent cited cost as their reason for not having an ombudsman, and another 8 percent said they were using other means to achieve the ombudsman's goals.) Peter S. Prichard, editor of *USA Today*, told Lauer: "We feel the editor, if he or she is doing the job properly, should have the responsibilities of an ombudsman."

Allan M. Siegal, assistant managing editor of the *New York Times*, said: "We do not believe the editors of this newspaper should abrogate their responsibility to deal with complaints of readers."

John M. Lemmon, managing editor of the *Baltimore Sun*, said: "All editors should be ombudsmen. Newspapers should not shirk this responsibility and cop out by appointing someone else to take the heat."

The simple defect of the "I'm the ombudsman" response is that the editor does not have time to be the ombudsman. The reader's representative at the *Minneapolis Tribune* averaged 17 contacts a day in one test period. That's about 4,000 calls or letters per year, and the mandate is to see that each of those questioners gets an answer. Top editors are and must be in many meetings each day. That leaves precious little time to call a questioner back. The simple test of the "I'm the ombudsman" editor is to try to reach him or her with a question about a story. On a big paper, it's not easy.

According to Ralph Langer, executive editor of the *Dallas Morning News*, the concept of "editor as ombudsman" means that the editor must set an atmosphere that will "ensure that every staff member takes every reader complaint seriously and that every inquiry or complaint from the public is investigated and a response is forthcoming." That suggestion has some merit, but the fact is that most complaints come in bearing an overlay of personal anger, political bias, and unreasonable language. A good ombudsman trains himself or herself to overcome his own defensiveness and wipe away the ordure—frequently not revealing the name of the complainer—in order to present a clean, clear journalistic question to the editor or reporter. One of the best reporters at the *Minneapolis Tribune* said to an angry news source when the reader's representative function was established: "Let's not you and me fight; the ombudsman gets paid to judge these things. Let's turn it over to him."

Most ombudsmen write a weekly column about complaints. The column is not subject to the editor's veto, and the column gives rise to misunderstanding—even among some ombudsmen and other journalists—about what the ombudsman's fundamental responsibility is.

On April 18, 1981, executive editor Ben Bradlee of the *Washington Post* walked into the newsroom and shouted, "You ungrateful son of a bitch, I salute you."[10]

Bradlee was saluting Bill Green, the *Post* ombudsman who had been writing for 24-1/2 hours to produce a no-holds-barred analysis of what had gone wrong at the *Post*. Some set of mishaps had allowed the publication of a totally false story by a 24-year-old cub reporter six months earlier. The story painted a vivid picture of an adult injecting heroin into the vein of an 8-year-old addict named "Jimmy." Now the account had won a Pulitzer prize, but in reporting the award, the Associated Press had discovered discrepancies in the reporter's academic credentials. Under questioning at the *Post*, the reporter had admitted her story was a lie. The *Post* had returned the Pulitzer. Green's analysis of what had gone wrong started on page one and spread over three and one-half inside pages. It is a paradigm for self-criticism by a newspaper and is truly one of the most remarkable documents in American journalism.

Yet two months after the *Post's* exemplary *mea culpa*, the National News Council judged that the ombudsman's report had "ignored a critical failure by the ombudsman himself: As a bridge between the *Post* editors on the one side and the community and staff on the other, it was his responsibility to insist that an inquiry be made early on when suspicion that Jimmy was not real was expressed by many District of Columbia officials and other readers. He did not. Nor did he heed concerns of some staff members about the truth of the story until after (the reporter's) confession."[11]

How could a news ombudsman have performed in an exemplary fashion with his critical analysis of his paper's work and at the same time be blamed for a critical failure? The answer is that sometimes the ombudsman is tempted away from the fundamental task of representing the reader into the difficult field of press criticism. The temptation is enhanced by the fact that readers, some of whom ought to know better, expect press criticism from the ombudsman.

As an example, John S. Carroll, executive editor of the *Lexington (Ky.) Herald-Leader*, said in response to Lauer's survey: "Some years ago when our rivals in Louisville published an ombudsman's column regularly, I was always delighted at the way he attacked his own paper's credibility and very often used our paper's coverage as a 'good' example."

The fact is that the Louisville papers never did have an ombudsman's column. Herchenroeder was established, as were Donald (Casey) Jones at the *Kansas City Star* and John V.R. Bull at the *Philadelphia Inquirer*, as ombudsmen without columns. Norman Isaacs and Herchenroeder thought that one-on-one contacts with the staff would be a more efficient device for improving journalistic performance. The column to which Carroll referred was not an ombudsman's column at all but a column of press criticism by Robert Schulman in the *Louisville Times*.

Prof. Theodore Glasser, now at the Stanford department of journalism, assumed the ombudsman was also a press critic and annoyed some ombudsmen in 1986 by writing that the ombudsman "is to press criticism what Ann Landers is to psychology." With particular reference to the *Minneapolis Star Tribune*, Glasser sneered at the job as "press relations" masquerading as press criticism, and he said the ombudsman lacked the authority to get things done that was called for in Raskin's ombudsman proposal.[12]

But at best the ombudsman does not masquerade as a press critic, nor does he seek line authority. John Brown, ombudsman at the *Edmonton Journal*, replied to Glasser: "For the newspaper ombudsman to have power to order changes would be to usurp the function of the editor. The ombudsman's power lies in his ability to persuade his organization that he has a case, and freedom to express his views."[13]

Except for the *Courier-Journal*, the *Inquirer*, and the *Kansas City Star*, virtually all 39 North American ombudsmen write columns today. Thor Severson concluded during his experience as the first ombudsman at the *Sacramento Bee* that the column is the ombudsman's clout. At the *Minneapolis Tribune*, the trust first enjoyed by a senior staff member who was appointed ombudsman was enough to get quick responses to the complaints he took from readers. However, as the staff changed and grew, the responses slowed, and a column seemed the best way to restore the quickness of staff response. In the column a laggard editor might be exposed to embarrassment.

In his farewell column in the *Washington Post*, ombudsman Charles B. Seib said, "To be at all effective, the ombudsman must have the right of publication—that is, his paper must be willing to print what he writes about it, however critical. Sometimes he can use that right to repair damages or redress a balance."[14]

"Repair damages," "redress a balance": That is the language of representing the reader, not of press criticism. Seib's contract at the *Post* required him to write a regular column to be syndicated by the Washington Post Writers' Group. That column tended to be press criticism, and at the end of his time at the *Post* Seib said if he were to do it again he would not take on that responsibility.

One of Seib's successors, Richard Harwood, the only one of the *Post's* ombudsmen to be reappointed for a second term, does write press criticism. Harwood brings to his debunking—and occasional defense of the press—an unusual mixture of experience, scholarship, and a graceful prose style. But more times than not he does not write about specific reader complaints, and the emphasis on representing the reader seems to be missing. "That's because you don't see the memos we get, or you don't hear him answer the phone," said executive editor Ben Bradlee.[15]

The reason it is risky to turn the ombudsman—or the regional press council—loose in the field of press criticism is that there is no satisfactory frame of reference for press criticism. The leftist critics employ a sort of Marxist framework, and the rightists apply a kind of unreconstructed libertarianism. For the rest, press criticism (or "commentary," which is the better word for what appears in newspapers and magazines of general circulation) uses as its frame of reference, when it has one at all, a vague concept of "good journalistic practice." This ideal is imperfectly captured in the codes of national news organizations (*i.e.*, the American Society of Newspaper Editors, Associated Press Managing Editors Association, Society of Professional Journalists, and the Radio-Television News Directors Association) and in the codes of individual newspapers, broadcast news networks, and individual stations.

It is important to note that the national codes, while imperfect, go back to the early part of the century. They are the product of that same journalistic honor on which we must still rely for any improvement in resolving conflicts with the press, or of going the next step to a creative dialogue between the press and the public. As early as 1908 Walter Williams, dean of the nation's first journalism school at Missouri, said there had been a diminution of the sense of journalism as a public trust. The first code was established by the Kansas Editorial Association in 1910. The ASNE codified its Canons of Journalism in 1923; SPJ its code in 1926.

But codes, particularly national codes, tend to alarm editors. John Siegenthaler, editorial page editor of *USA Today* and editor of the *Nashville Tennessean*, said in a 1987 workshop on press ethics: "The only code of conduct I need is the Constitution of the United States and of my state of Tennessee." Most editors are more circumspect, but many share Siegenthaler's disenchantment with national codes because the codes cannot cover all cases. And, their lawyers tell the editors, there is a danger that the standards of conduct established by such codes might be used successfully in a lawsuit to demonstrate that the newspaper had not lived up to accepted standards of journalistic conduct in a particular case.

Because of these fears the organizations have not enforced their codes. In 1924 Frederick G. Bonfils accepted $1 million in oil stock not to publish the news his *Denver Post* had discovered about the illegal sale of oil reserves from the Teapot Dome oilfield. It was a clear violation of the Canons, yet after three years of indecision the ASNE declined to throw out Bonfils because to do so would interfere with the freedom of the press. This is the same editors' organization that

40 years later was to defy the efforts of Norman Isaacs, then its president, to establish a grievance committee. And the reluctance to enforce is not limited to editors. In 1986 the Society of Professional Journalists damaged itself, perhaps irreparably, by listening to its lawyers and voting down an effort to enforce its own code.

Ironically, the news divisions of the broadcast networks, whose ethics are viewed with scorn by print journalists, do have detailed and useful codes to guide their reporting. When Gen. William Westmoreland challenged the fairness of CBS News' documentary "The Uncounted Enemy," CBS News senior executive producer Burton Benjamin reviewed the preparation of the documentary and found it had violated the CBS code in a number of specifics. It is another example of journalistic honor manifesting itself that the ethical codes of CBS News, NBC News, and PBS station WGBH-TV in Boston are the product of one man, Richard Salant, who was at one time or another an executive of each organization.

Most press codes could be improved by untangling three elements and framing on one newsroom wall the ideals to which a journalist might aspire but could not be penalized for not reaching. On another piece of paper would be listed the clear offenses—lying, plagiarism, hidden conflict of interest—for which a journalist must be punished. For the rest—the day-to-day questions like whether to break a pledge of confidentiality, whether to use a stolen document, whether to cooperate with police in an investigation, whether to use a dramatic but heart-breaking picture, how far to intrude on a person's privacy— these questions should be left to be worked out by editors on a day-to-day basis, and to be discussed by ombudsmen and regional press councils on a case-by-case basis.

But such issues should not be discussed as they tend to be now, *i.e.*, without any clear frame of reference or system of ethical analysis. Journalists need to abandon the defensiveness exhibited by Siegenthaler and adopt one of a number of systems of ethical analysis that will force them to balance certain clearly stated values in making journalistic decisions. In his book *The Reluctant Reformation*, Lee Brown says: "Criticism should be realistic in that response is possible and guidance is offered. Its values must precede the criticism;

both must be public. It should mediate actual ideal values of the press and the public."[16]

Edmund Lambeth has suggested five values against which to measure the ethics of journalistic actions. They are Freedom, Justice, Truthfulness, Humaneness, and Stewardship of the news medium.[17] If journalists made decisions with reference to those values, they would not necessarily make unanimous decisions, nor would their decisions necessarily win approval from the public. However, they would find that they could answer complaints from the public in terms that the public can understand. Readers know what it is to preserve freedom. Readers know what it is to be fair. Readers know what it is to tell the truth or keep a promise. Readers know what it means to do no harm. And readers know what it means to want to preserve or improve the reputation of the news media we have inherited.

It is not difficult today to find teachers to train working journalists in ethical analysis. It is not difficult to demonstrate the inadequacies of Immanuel Kant or John Stuart Mill as managing editors. Nor is it difficult to find in Aristotle a practical guide to discover and clarify values. Medicine, to name one profession, has had to develop specific systems for making life-and-death ethical decisions. Some of these systems prove useful when they are applied to journalistic dilemmas.

Without some such approach to ethical analysis, the best decisions of ombudsmen and news councils will continue to seem superficial. An example: The National News Council adjudicated a complaint that two women whose identity could not be hidden in their small town, even though their names were not used, had been heartlessly exposed by the reporting of each sordid detail of their rapes as revealed in a pretrial hearing. The news council took the position that it must not seem to criticize the accurate reporting of material laid out in open court.[18] Why not, for goodness sake? To limit oneself so is to become legalistic. Why not balance compassion against the freedom to publish? And, if one of the purposes of the publication was to frighten citizens into locking their doors, why not balance that value against the value of fairness as it applied to publishing the details without consulting the women? All hands might not agree on the weight each value should be given, but to discuss the case in value terms at the news council—and better yet at the newspapers—gives such decisions more ethical clout and, one can hope, may result in better reporting.

The judgment in a recent Minnesota News Council case is somewhat less superficial.[19] The council considered whether a television station ought to have sent a reporter posing as a participant and concealing a camera to a training meeting of a self-improvement group. The council said: "Deceptive surveillance, which might be condemned if done by the government, is generally permitted by the news media. (True? The *Chicago Sun-Times* was denied a Pulitzer prize because it used deception to develop an expose of bribery among city building inspectors.) The council said: "Generally speaking there must be some serious question of the legitimacy of a particular enterprise to justify the use of deception in obtaining information." And it concluded: "In this case, it seems to us that sufficient controversy surrounded the self-improvement program to warrant the reporter's ostensible enrollment in the training course and to use a camera to report on the activity." The council did say that the invasion of people's privacy with a camera raises serious ethical concerns, but it said the impact was lessened in this case by the television station's "blurring the picture images so no one was identifiable."

Whether one agrees or not with the council's decision, the only values one gets to weigh in deciding whether the station should have used deception were "legitimacy" and "controversy"; there is no assessment of the impact of deception, for example, on the reporter, the station, the people involved in the workshop, or the community as a whole. And for the privacy issue, the decision dismisses the special interest of the innocent participants in the meeting by saying the television station blurred their pictures. What about the unblurred film? Who's got it? Who can look at it? What about trust in the reporter, the station, in the news council itself that my privacy won't be secretly invaded and the invasion approved next week?

Ombudsmen fall even shorter than news councils in using ethical analysis to judge journalistic actions. Their columns reflect the lack of ethical analysis in the newsrooms from which they come.

Ombudsmen do refer—usually by implication—to values like fairness, compassion, and privacy in their judgments of cases over time, but it is rare to see a column in which an ombudsman makes a judgment on one or more clearly stated ethical values. Because it is so rare, a column by Henry McNulty, reader's representative at the *Hartford Courant*, stands out. McNulty acknowledged that the *Courant* had performed a useful service by exposing racial bias among real estate people. But, he said, the usefulness was outweighed by a single factor: Reporters had masqueraded as clients to get the story. That was dishonest, and McNulty said the impact of the dishonesty on the paper and the community outweighed the good of the expose.[20]

That's good and clear, and it doesn't take a Ph.D. in ethics to make such judgments. The further ombudsmen and news councils go in using ethical values, the further the press and the public can go toward a realistic dialogue on the processes and functions of the press.

The dialogue is more likely to turn up commonly held values at the community level than at the national level—or in the courts. Prof. Hugh Stevenson of the University of London has now taken the post of ombudsman on one of Great Britain's national newspapers, but he believes that the ombudsman position is more appropriate, both in Great Britain and the United States, for newspapers that are not national.[21] He says the non-national newspapers and their ombudsmen are themselves citizens of the community, and therefore more likely to agree on community values. Richard Salant agreed; he said it was this lack of a sense of citizenship in a national community with shared values that got in the way of establishing an effective ombudsman operation for CBS News.[22] It is certainly true that the local journalist, the local news council member, and the local ombudsman are more likely to reflect commonly held values than is the ombudsman of a national news organization because the national values are no longer particularly clear. But there is a danger here. In dialogue over community values, the press representatives must be prepared to defend—in value terms—their obligation to report the news; community members may initially give less weight to the journalist's obligation to bear witness to unpleasant truths.

It is unlikely that other state or regional councils will arise and assume jurisdiction over all the news media in their area, as the Minnesota News Council did. Since the formation of the Minnesota News Council, the publishers in two states, Wisconsin and Kentucky, have voted against the formation of state councils. In each case the seed of honor that did germinate in Minnesota was killed by strong opponents who played on the innate defensiveness of fence-straddling editors to kill the proposals. As a matter of historic fact, the council would not have been started in Minnesota if the publishers association had taken a vote. A few editors with the support of the Minneapolis *Star* and *Tribune*, the biggest newspapers in the state, simply went ahead and did it.

Therefore, the best hope for expansion of the news council idea is for the Minnesota News Council to "go national" and hear complaints against out-of-state news organizations, or for new state and regional news councils to be formed. In both instances the participation of news organizations should be voluntary, as in the Canadian model. Some threat to freedom of the press may be necessary to nudge American editors. That was the case in the formation of the Press Council in Great Britain. But it is difficult to conceive of such a threat in light of the First Amendment, and it would be too bad if that were necessary. News organizations that committed themselves voluntarily would be committing to a creative project that would expand their understanding of their own communities and increase community understanding of the journalistic process. Unwilling editors, on the other hand, would approach the news councils narrowly and legalistically.

If this process goes ahead—and the key word is "voluntarily"—we will see news organizations that have voluntarily established ombudsmen and have voluntarily joined together in regional news councils. We may even see groups of individuals, discouraged by the failure of SPJ to enforce its code, joining together in local organizations and committing themselves publicly to a set of simple values and promising to answer complaints in public hearings when someone believes their performance has fallen short.

By so doing those newspapers and those journalists would differentiate themselves from others who do not commit to the same standards. And in the dialogue over specific complaints with ombudsmen and news councils[23] we can hope not only for a clarification of journalistic values, but for the rediscovery of commonly held community values.

In his 1963 book, *Social Responsibility of the Press*, J. Edward Gerald spoke of conflict between society's complaints about the press and the resistance to that criticism on the part of the "subculture of journalism." He said:

> A sort of dialogue between the press and society ensues, one part of which reveals keen anxiety about the adequacy of our basic social control structure. It is from this anxiety that criticism of press performance arises. The author shares that anxiety and looks upon the press as the one social institution in a position to help renovate and perpetuate the system of personal values which, taken in the aggregate, make free society possible.[24]

Complaints against the press reflect community attitudes. Community attitudes do change from time to time and from place to place. Today, for example, it is shocking to read the patronizing view of William Allen White, the revered publisher of the *Emporia (Kan.) Gazette*, on the publication of information he didn't think the community needed to know. Dialogue in value language conducted by ombudsmen and community news councils would reflect changes in community attitudes without the necessity of new language: What changes when attitudes change is not the values, but the weight that each is given. Therefore, the ombudsman and the community news council can be forums in which community values remain clear as attitudes change.

Notes

[1] A thorough and insightful description of the founding and first 10 years of the Minnesota council was offered in 1982 by Robert M. Schafer. ("The Minnesota Press Council," unpublished Master's thesis, University of Minnesota, Minneapolis, Minn., 1982.) Schafer is now an associate managing editor at the *Minneapolis Star Tribune*.

[2] As an example, Louise W. Hermanson, assistant professor of communication at the University of South Alabama, Mobile, Ala., has done research that will be valuable to the Minnesota News Council and to future councils on the reactions of complainants to the handling of their complaints. See, for instance, her essay in this book at Chapter 1, pp. 15–41.

[3] Paine, Sylvia, "The Minnesota News Council," *Washington Journalism Review*, Vol. 11, No. 9, Nov. 1989, pp. 24,25.

[4] Letter to the council, June 25, 1990, from Karen Christensen, assistant general counsel of National Public Radio: "While the News Council appears to have an impressive and commendable history in Minnesota, we do not believe that the News Council is an appropriate forum for resolution of this complaint against NPR."

[5] Telephone interview with Louise W. Hermanson, Aug. 1, 1990.

[6] Information on the Canadian councils is from Mel Sufrin, executive secretary of the Ontario Press Council.

[7] The number of ombudsmen does not appear so meager when one looks at the circulations of newspapers that have them. Mike Clark, reader's advocate for the *Florida Times-Union*, reported in his May 27, 1990, column: "Of the top 100 circulation newspapers in the United States, 27 have positions like the reader advocate." A 1983 study by Clair Balfour, ombudsman at the *Gazette* in Montreal, showed that there were ombudsmen on United States and Canadian daily newspapers with circulations totaling 6,288,430 weekdays and 11,448,056 weekends.

[8] Raskin, A.H., "What's wrong with American newspapers," *New York Times Magazine*, June 11, 1967, p. 28.

[9] An investigation by White killed a whole genre of stories about ships' cats. He noticed that in each of the stories about a series of shipwrecks there was mention of the rescue of the ship's cat. White asked a *World* reporter if all ships carried cats. The reporter confessed that in the first of the wrecks there was indeed a ship's cat, and the crew went back to save it. The reporter featured the incident

THE STATE NEWS COUNCIL AND THE OMBUDSMAN   63

in his story, and competitive reporters were assailed by their city editors for missing the cat. In the next shipwreck there was no cat, but all the reporters except the *World's* put one in just to be safe. The *World* reporter said: "I was severely chided for being beaten. Now when there is a shipwreck, all of us always put in a cat." (*American* Magazine, Nov. 1916.)

[10] *After 'Jimmy's World': Tightening Up in Editing*, (New York: National News Council, 1981), p. 110.

[11] *Ibid.*, p. 61.

[12] Glasser, Theodore, "Why the Star and Tribune should do something crazy," *Twin Cities*, April 1986, p. 91.

[13] Brown, John, [Letter to the editor], *Journalism Quarterly*, Vol. 65, No. 1, Spring 1988, p. 254. The letter responded to the same point made by Glasser in Ettema, James S. and Glasser, Theodore, "Public accountability or public relations? Newspaper ombudsmen define their role," *Journalism Quarterly*, Vol. 64, No. 1, Spring 1987, p. 3.

[14] Seib, Charles B., "Having watched the watchdog," *Washington Post*, Nov. 9, 1979, p. A21.

[15] Telephone interview, Oct. 16, 1989.

[16] Brown, Lee, *The Reluctant Reformation*, (New York: McKay Co., 1974), p. 19.

[17] Lambeth, Edmund B., *Committed Journalism*, (Bloomington: University of Indiana Press, 1984), pp. 29-39.

[18] Case No. 195, *In the Public Interest—III*, (New York: National News Council, 1983), p. 324.

[19] Minnesota News Council Determination No. 83, *Lifespring, Inc. v. KARE-TV*, July 30, 1990.

[20] McNulty, Henry, "Real estate probe built on deception," *Hartford Courant*, June 4, 1989, p. D3.

[21] Interview, London, Oct. 19, 1989.

[22] Telephone interview, Aug. 1, 1990.

[23] Based on the history of community press councils founded on improving race relations or interests other than the hearing of complaints, the complaint-based

council is the only form worth considering. Discussions of the fate of other kinds of councils can be found in Rivers, *et al*, *Backtalk*, (San Francisco: Canfield, 1972); Brown, Lee, *The Reluctant Reformation*, (New York: McKay Co., 1974); and *A Free and Responsive Press*, (New York: The Twentieth Century Fund, 1973).

[24] Gerald, J. Edward, *Social Responsibility of the Press*, (Minneapolis: University of Minnesota Press, 1963), p. 101.

III. A Proposal for Libel Law Reform
Richard M. Schmidt, Jr.

The thorny, complex issue of libel law in the United States—how it works and where it fails—was studied and debated by a special task force assembled under the auspices of The Annenberg Washington Program. Working through the winter of 1987-88, 11 members of the Libel Reform Project represented a wide variety of backgrounds and viewpoints.

The report resulting from their deliberations in 1988 is a proposal for the reform of libel law.[1]

The Annenberg Program

Now in its eighth year, The Annenberg Washington Program in Communications Policy Studies of Northwestern University was established in 1983. Its mission has been to assess how communications technologies and today's public policies on communications affect many aspects of American life including education, medicine, law, politics, foreign policy, and financial markets. The Annenberg Program provides a neutral forum for diverse opinion and examination of how well current policies serve the public interest.

Newton N. Minow, a well-known Chicago and Washington, D.C., attorney who was chairman of the Federal Communications Commission during the Kennedy administration, serves as director of the Annenberg Program. The Libel Reform Project was conceived by Minow. "His hypothesis was that the current libel system is not working well for anyone," the 1988 report cites as Minow's reason for creating the project. "It neither adequately protects First Amendment values nor provides plaintiffs with an effective way to vindicate their damaged reputations. Plaintiffs, defendants, judges, and academics have all criticized the modern law of libel. Minow proposed to bring together a group of thoughtful experts from various libel 'constituencies' for an extended exploration of the current system."[2]

With the possible exception of some segments of the legal profession, no one has been very happy with the present state of libel law in this country. America's journalists in particular have been all too aware of libel law problems, but plaintiffs, defendants, judges, academicians, and everyone else who has come into contact with the system agree that it is not working well for anyone.

While earlier studies by the University of Iowa and the Libel Defense Resource Center show that plaintiffs in libel cases who sue the media have an excellent chance of victory before a jury, the vast majority of those jury awards are reversed either by the trial judge or an appellate court.

It is also true that libel suits can be enormously expensive for both sides, often costing parties and their insurance companies hundreds of thousands, and even millions, of dollars.

Who Participated

Rodney A. Smolla, director of the Institute of Bill of Rights Law at the College of William and Mary Law School, was the director of the project. He is a nationally recognized constitutional authority and author of several books on libel.[3]

The other members of the project represented a wide spectrum of expertise in the fields of law and communications:

- Sandra S. Baron, managing general attorney in the law department of the National Broadcasting Company. She is responsible for legal matters involving NBC News.
- Bruce E. Fein, nationally known conservative legal commentator and former general counsel to the Federal Communications Commission.
- Judge Lois G. Forer, a retired judge of the Court of Common Pleas in Philadelphia and an author on libel law.
- Samuel E. Klein, a libel defense attorney from Philadelphia. He has been actively engaged in all phases of First Amendment litigation.
- Anthony Lewis, a nationally known columnist for the *New York Times*, lecturer of law at Harvard Law School, and author of several books.
- Roslyn A. Mazer, a Washington, D.C., attorney who has devoted much of her practice to First Amendment cases.
- Chad E. Milton, vice president and assistant general counsel for Media/Professional Insurance, Inc., the nation's largest underwriter of media insurance.
- Anthony S. Murry, an attorney with the U.S. Department of Justice, Civil Rights Division, who played a key role in the *Westmoreland v. CBS, Inc.* libel trial as one of the principal lawyers for the plaintiff.
- Herbert Schmertz, former vice president of Mobil Oil Corp., who became particularly interested in libel issues through his role at Mobil during the celebrated case of *Tavoulareas v. Washington Post Co.*
- Richard M. Schmidt, Jr., the author of this article, a Washington communications lawyer who has served as general counsel of the American Society of Newspaper Editors and Washington counsel for the Association of American Publishers, Inc. since 1969.

Background

Several widely publicized cases in recent years have made the public aware of the problems inherent in the current libel law system. In General Westmoreland's libel suit against CBS both sides spent millions of dollars and months in trial only to see the suit terminated just before it was sent to the jury, with both sides joining in a public statement. Another celebrated trial, which pitted Israeli General Ariel Sharon against *Time* Magazine, ended in a technical victory for the publication but with both sides claiming the jury had vindicated their reputations.

When the president of Mobil Oil, William Tavoulareas, sued the *Washington Post* he received a jury award of $2 million—which just covered his attorneys' fees. The award was finally reversed by an appellate court—after much legal maneuvering—and again, each side claimed its position had been vindicated by the jury. Television star Carol Burnett sued the *National Enquirer* which had erroneously reported that the actress had made a spectacle of herself at a restaurant after an evening of drinking. The *National Enquirer* printed a retraction which was held legally insufficient under California law. After years of legal proceedings and untold millions in legal fees, the litigation was settled without disclosure of the terms of settlement. The cost of appealing a multi-million-dollar jury award in a case involving a small newspaper in downstate Illinois, the *Alton Telegraph*, eventually forced the paper into bankruptcy.

These cases among others were studied by the project members who often drew on their personal experiences as well. They recognized that libel suits are often prohibitively expensive for both plaintiffs and defendants and tend to drag on interminably. Current libel law also presents judges in these cases with extremely complex problems in applying pertinent law.

In many cases the issue of truth or falsity is never litigated. As the executive summary of the report states:

> Libel suits only occasionally resolve the most critical issue from the plaintiff's perspective, whether the defamatory statement was true or false. The litigation often focuses on the

defendant's alleged malice or recklessness rather than on the question of truth. This not only leaves many plaintiffs unsatisfied but also undercuts one of the great purposes of the First Amendment—encouraging the dissemination of truth in the marketplace of ideas through robust and uncensored debate. After years of litigation, the court either fails to set the record straight or does too late for the decision to be meaningful or useful.[4]

The Report

The preamble to the proposed Libel Reform Act states: "The purpose of this Act is to provide an efficient and speedy remedy for defamation, emphasizing the compelling public interest in the dissemination of truth in the marketplace. The provisions of this Act are intended to encourage the prompt resolution of defamation disputes through remedies other than money damages and should be liberally construed to accomplish that purpose."[5]

The Reform Act creates a new premise for libel law—that its ultimate purpose is the timely dissemination of truth. The proposal eliminates any distinctions between media and non-media defendants which currently prevail in many jurisdictions. It also creates one cause of action—for defamation for all claims based on publication of false defamatory statements. The act further curtails the use of other legal strategies to avoid the rules of the act, eliminating a major alternative cause of action often used by litigants to evade rules of libel trials such as false-light invasion of privacy.

Retraction or Right of Reply

The libel project members, after prolonged discussion, reached a consensus on proposed ground rules which if adopted, they feel, will lead to a simplification of the system, greater justice, and significantly lower costs of litigation.

Under the libel reform provisions every plaintiff would be required to seek a retraction or an opportunity to reply before filing suit. Additionally:

- If the defendant subsequently honors the plaintiff's request within 30 days, no suit may be brought.
- If the plaintiff demands a retraction, the defendant can avoid litigation only by publishing a retraction. The proposed act defines a retraction as "...a good faith publication of facts, withdrawing and repudiating the prior defamatory statements."
- If the plaintiff demands an opportunity to reply, the defendant can avoid litigation either by granting the plaintiff a chance to reply or by publishing a retraction. Under the provision of the act a reply is defined as "...the publication of the plaintiff's statement of the facts."

Requirements governing the timing, placement, and format of retractions and replies are set forth in the proposal. For example, a request for a retraction or reply must be made in writing and signed by the complainant or his or her authorized attorney or agent. It must specify the statements claimed to be false and defamatory and must set forth the plaintiff's version of the facts. If the request is for a retraction and the defendant decides to make a retraction it must be timely and conspicuous. A conspicuous retraction is one that is published in substantially the same place and manner as the defamatory statements being retracted. It must be reasonably calculated to reach the same audience as the prior defamatory statements being retracted. If the request by the plaintiff is for an opportunity to reply and the defendant grants the request, it must be a conspicuous and timely opportunity to reply. A conspicuous reply is one written by the plaintiff and published in substantially the same place and manner as the defamatory statements to which the reply is directed.

In the case of a broadcast, the defendant may require that the reply not exceed the length of the defamatory material broadcast and that its form reasonably accommodate the nature of the medium in which it is to be broadcast. The reply must be concise and limited to rebuttal of the defamatory statements.

The requirement that all plaintiffs demand a retraction or chance to reply before bringing suit is based on the assumption that a retraction or opportunity to reply will restore most plaintiffs' reputations as quickly and cheaply as possible. The public record is thereby corrected expeditiously—or benefits, at least, from a full airing of the plaintiff's view. Should the plaintiff ask for a retraction, the defendant knows that granting one will instantly end the dispute. In the opinion of the project members, this would serve as a powerful incentive for the defendant to pay attention to the plaintiff's demand and issue a timely retraction—certainly most likely in those cases where the defendant determines that a mistake has indeed been made.

The project report recognizes that in some instances the plaintiff may proceed to sue, contending that the retraction or opportunity to reply does not meet the requirements of the act. This then becomes the first issue considered by the court. If the court decides the retraction or opportunity to reply is adequate, the case is ended and the plaintiff becomes liable for the attorneys' fees of the defendant.

Even if the defendant stands by the original story and refuses to retract, the act still gives both sides an incentive to negotiate and bargain. In this case, the defendant could see fit to offer the plaintiff an opportunity to reply. The act thereby encourages the parties to negotiate at the start of the dispute instead of going through months and years of expensive litigation which may simply end with an agreement on the wording of a joint public statement.

It should be kept in mind that the act gives the plaintiff an absolute right to demand a retraction in the first instance. Should it be unclear whether the plaintiff has demanded a retraction or a reply, the act provides that the request is to be construed as a request for a retraction. Under the provisions of the act, a plaintiff who demands a retraction may not be sidetracked by the defendant who offers a right of reply. However, if the plaintiff requests a right of reply, the defendant may avoid litigation by providing either the opportunity to reply or by publishing a retraction. There is obviously no need for a reply if the defendant has voluntarily retracted the defamation.

To meet the standards set forth in the act, a retraction must repudiate the published defamatory statements and publish the corrected facts. An equivocal or hypothetical retraction will not suffice. If the allegedly defamatory statement is not a statement actually published by the defendant but an implication communicated by the actual statements, the defendant may satisfy the retraction requirement by publishing the fact that the defendant did not intend either to state or imply the meaning ascribed by the plaintiff.

If the plaintiff does not obtain a retraction or an opportunity to reply, the parties may then proceed to litigation. At this point, either side may dictate that the suit will be tried as an action for declaratory judgment.

Declaratory Judgment

While both sides pay a price, they also receive benefits. By choosing a declaratory judgment, the plaintiff will not have a chance to collect money damages while the defendant will not enjoy all of the current First Amendment rules for protection. But, both sides get a quicker trial and probably one they can afford. Declaratory judgment trials are normally less expensive than damage trials and usually must begin within 120 days after the suit is filed.

In a declaratory suit, the only issue to be litigated is the truth or falsity of the defamatory statement. The only money paid by the loser is the fee of the winner's attorney. Project members believe that the declaratory judgment option set forth in the Reform Act can be compared to an auto claim under no-fault insurance. The defendant's knowledge, recklessness, negligence, or malice are not issues, and who was at fault is irrelevant. The only question to be decided is whether the statement at issue was true or false.

The plaintiff, by opting for the declaratory judgment, can force the defendant to surrender the fault standards that tend to make it extremely difficult to ultimately win a suit for damages under the current system. But, while a successful plaintiff surrenders the chance of receiving damages, he or she will not have to pay attorneys' fees and at the same time will prevail as to the issue of truth or falsity.

This will also be accomplished on a far more rapid timetable than under the current system.

The declaratory judgment should also be attractive from the defendant's standpoint, for those against whom the suit was filed are immunized against liability for money damages; if they are confident of their publication, they can get a quick verdict and recover attorneys' fees as well. While it is true that the defendant would lose the protection of First Amendment fault standards that apply in a suit for money damages, it is thought that many defendants would exercise a declaratory judgment option to avoid the possibility of large money damage awards.

Additionally, a declaratory judgment remedy is more likely to restore the injured reputation at a time when it really counts—shortly after publication of the alleged libel.

As far as the public interest is concerned, a judicial declaration of truth that comes from a trial which must begin within 120 days after the suit is filed is done at a far lower cost to society than the traditional suit for damages. The incentive to settle is increased because of the risk the loser bears of having to pay the other side's legal fees.

Money Damages

The next course of action, if neither side takes the declaratory judgment option, is to move to an action for money damages. These suits will in most aspects be along the lines of current libel actions for money damages with each side paying its own attorneys' fees, but with the further proviso that the plaintiff will be awarded only actual damages. "Presumed" and "punitive" damages are eliminated in the proposal.

Currently many winning plaintiffs are entitled to "presumed damages," which are those awarded without any proof of actual injury. "Punitive damages" are those designed to punish and deter the defendant rather than to compensate the plaintiff. Punitive awards often bear no relation to reality and may operate more to express distaste for the nature or character of the defendant than to serve any rational interest.

Opinion

The proposed act seeks to prevent plaintiffs from suing because they object to statements of opinion, including hyperbole and ridicule. It presumes that editorials, letters to the editor, editorial cartoons, reviews, parody, satire, and fiction are works of opinion. Current legal tests used to define fact and opinion are often confusing.

In determining whether the statements giving rise to the litigation are defamatory statements of fact or statements of opinion, the act provides that the court and trier-of-fact shall consider:
  (1) the extent to which the statements are objectively verifiable or provable;
  (2) the extent to which the statements were made in a context in which they were likely to be reasonably understood as opinion or rhetorical hyperbole and not as statements of fact; and
  (3) the language used, including its common meaning, and the extent to which qualifying or cautionary language, or a disclaimer, was employed.

Truth or Falsity

Under provisions of the proposal, the plaintiff shall bear the burden of proving by clear and convincing evidence that the defamatory statements are false, whether the action is one for declaratory judgment or damages. It further provides that the plaintiff does *not* meet this burden if the defamatory statements are substantially true. This constitutes a codification of the common law.

Minimum Fault Requirements

The act provides that in all defamation actions for damages, the plaintiff bears the burden of proving, through clear and convincing evidence, that the defendant failed to act as a reasonable person under the circumstances.

The U.S. Supreme Court has ruled under the First Amendment that where public officials or public figures bring an action for defamation they must prove the defendant published the defamatory statement with knowledge of falsity or reckless disregard for truth or falsity.[6] This constitutional requirement cannot be amended by statute. Therefore the act establishes negligence as the universal minimum statutory fault level, but does not attempt to codify the higher levels of fault required by the Supreme Court through constitutional adjudication.

Neutral Reportage

The act also adopts a "neutral reportage" privilege. This would eliminate suits against defendants quoting someone else when the source is identified, when the quote involves a matter of public interest, and when the statement is accurately quoted. In this event a plaintiff's recourse is an action against the person who made the defamatory statements.

Privilege

An absolute privilege for statements made by participants in judicial and legislative proceedings is established by the act. This includes executive and administrative proceedings that are quasi-judicial or quasi-legislative in character. Public hearings before agencies such as school boards are within the scope of the privilege. These absolute privileges allow unfettered freedom of speech in certain narrowly defined settings.

This is allowed because these settings are subject to the truth-seeking devices of the judicial or legislative processes and serve to vindicate the public interest in the dissemination of truth in the marketplace; the need for defamation actions to serve that function is thereby diminished. Obviously the public need for complete candor and openness by participants in governmental proceedings is a necessity that must prevail over any private interest or the vindication of reputation.

Libel or Slander

The obsolete distinction between libel (written defamation) and slander (oral defamation) is eliminated in the act. Modern forms of technology have blurred the distinction between oral and written communication, but unfortunately under current law, different damage rules apply to the two forms of defamation suits.

Reaction

Reaction to the Annenberg report was immediate and intense, particularly from those engaged in the defense of libel suits on behalf of the media.

Harry M. Johnston, III, vice president and general counsel of Time Inc. Magazine Company, and Henry R. Kaufman, chairman and general counsel of the Libel Defense Resource Center, wrote in the publication *Communications Lawyer*:

> The Annenberg report is probably the most thoughtful and complete of the recent spate of libel law reform proposals. Its attempt to find common ground among representatives of both plaintiffs and defendants is certainly commendable. Many of the discrete reforms embodied in the report are clearly long overdue. If considered individually, these might well find enthusiastic support, at least among representatives of the media. But despite these positive aspects, we find ourselves convinced that the Annenberg proposals as a whole lack merit.[7]

The proposal for a declaratory judgment procedure was criticized by Johnston and Kaufman. They pointed out that media representatives opposed similar measures, one proposed by Rep. Charles Schumer (D-New York), and others introduced in the California and Illinois legislatures. Johnston and Kaufman raised the possibility that mandatory declaratory judgments may well be unconstitutional.

They also expressed the fear that if the act were introduced in state legislatures, it could be radically changed for the worse from a First

Amendment point of view by legislators who are not motivated by admiration of the media. They called for a program to pursue judicial reform on a case-by-case basis of the problems inherent in libel law.

"If the thrust of the proposed Libel Reform Act was to be provocative, it has achieved that goal," wrote *Boston Globe* ombudsman Robert L. Kierstead.[8]

In his *Globe* article Kierstead quoted Professor Gilbert Cranberg of the University of Iowa and former editorial page editor of the *Des Moines Register*, who feels the proposal should be of great interest to editors.

"Under the present damages system, a newspaper gets dissected, its operation scrutinized in the courts. Newspapers should shudder at this intrusion. The issue of whether something is true or false becomes almost secondary," Cranberg said.

Jane Kirtley, executive director of the Reporters Committee for Freedom of the Press, was quoted in the *Christian Science Monitor*[9]: "News organizations should not be put in the position of having to respond [to a libel plaintiff to avoid trial]. Retraction or reply should be voluntary."

In the same article Everette Dennis, who heads the Gannett Center for Media Studies at Columbia University, praised the Annenberg project for "the courage of putting this on the table."

The *National Law Journal* editorialized that the Annenberg proposal tries to make the system more responsive to plaintiffs' legitimate desires to quickly rehabilitate their reputations while removing much of the financial exposure of media defendants.

"Such radical reform will almost certainly encounter serious resistance," the editorial concluded. "Nonetheless, the proposals—with their emphasis on negotiation and retraction—may help point us out of the dead-end of current libel litigation."[10]

The *American Bar Association Journal* quoted Floyd Abrams, well-known First Amendment advocate. The Annenberg proposal is "valuable, innovative, and very constructive," Abrams said. While there may be a serious question as to its constitutionality, it is "well worthy of a try-out," he added.[11]

Don Reuben, counsel to the *Chicago Tribune*, was also quoted by the *ABA Journal*. Seeing the proposal as hardest on reporters, Reuben said: "Publishers will have less of a motivation to pump a lot of money and effort into defending these cases. Once reporters realize this, there will be a chilling effect."

The concerns expressed by critics that the determination of "truth or falsity" is a difficult task and that the proposal might lead to an increase in frivolous litigation are certainly worthy of consideration. However, the answers to these concerns cannot be determined by speculation alone. Fears of legislative tampering with the proposal may also have merit. But those who advocate a case-by-case approach to reform in this area overlook the fact that the broad proposals set forth in the Annenberg proposal cannot and will not be accomplished by judicial decisions. If such reform is to be achieved under our system it must come from legislative action.

Another critic of the Annenberg proposal was U.S. District Judge Pierre N. Leval, who was the presiding judge in the celebrated libel trial *Westmoreland v. CBS, Inc.* The Annenberg panel had studied Judge Leval's article in the *Harvard Law Review*[12] advocating the use of declaratory judgment suits in libel cases in lieu of actions for money damages. This article was in reality the genesis of the Annenberg proposal for the use of the declaratory judgment procedure. However, Judge Leval, in correspondence with project director Rodney Smolla and in a personal appearance at a seminar on the project report, pointed out that under his proposal the plaintiff's participation in a declaratory judgment action would be voluntary and the plaintiff could not be forced into such action by the action of the defendant. Judge Leval criticized the Annenberg proposal's provisions for retraction and reply and other factors as unfair to libel plaintiffs.

Thus the Annenberg proposal has been viewed by some as pro defense and by others as pro plaintiff.

Recently Michael Traynor, a practicing lawyer in San Francisco and a lecturer at Boalt Hall School of Law, University of California at Berkeley, authored an article in the *Journal of College and University Law*[13] concerning the case of *Neary v. Regents of the University of California*.[14] In this case, a jury awarded $7 million in damages to a rancher who sued a university and three of its veterinarians for defamation. A public report blaming the rancher and absolving the state for the deaths of the rancher's cattle provoked the lawsuit. Traynor writes that the case is pending on appeal but "[w]hatever the eventual result, both sides already have suffered economic and reputational harm."

If the verdict is affirmed it will be 10 times larger than any libel verdict ever affirmed by a California appellate court, a fact that has already "jolted research institutions," Traynor notes. The article states that the verdict in *Neary* may motivate legislatures, courts, and researchers themselves to take a new look at defamation law. It cites the Annenberg proposal as a "good tool" available for such a "new look."

Referring to the Annenberg proposal,[15] Traynor states: "Defendants might consider offering to stipulate to a procedure such as that provided by the Libel Reform Act for determining truth. Neary's counsel states that Neary 'would have jumped at such an offer.' Letter from David Meadows of Keker & Brochett to Michael Traynor, dated September 14, 1989."

Rodney Smolla, director of the Annenberg project and the principal draftsman of its report, accomplished what many observers thought to be impossible—a consensus report from 11 widely ideologically diverse persons who represented plaintiffs, defendants, and the judiciary.

Writing in the *William and Mary Law Review*,[16] Smolla summed up the report:

> One can hardly imagine another area of American law so prone to intense and emotional posturing by the contending forces as libel law. Cool thinking is difficult in the charged atmosphere of libel reform debate. The Annenberg libel reform proposal requires both sides to take some leaps of faith. Plaintiffs must have faith that they can indeed be made whole—or at least substantially more whole than under current law—by a system that emphasizes counter-speech and the determination of truth rather than money damages.

Defendants must have faith that the Act will not encourage frivolous litigation, or create an Orwellian truth squad.

The tension between freedom of speech and freedom from unwarranted reputational attack will always exist. The Annenberg proposal is a creative attempt to make constructive use of that tension.

Smolla concludes: "The proposal is not perfect—no reform ever will be—but it is thoughtfully balanced and contains many provisions that improve significantly on the often perverse and irrational rules of existing law."

Notes

[1] *Proposal for the Reform of Libel Law: The Report of the Libel Reform Project of The Annenberg Washington Program*, (Washington: The Annenberg Washington Program in Communications Policy Studies of Northwestern University, 1988) [hereinafter cited as *Annenberg Proposal*].

[2] *Ibid.*, p. 7.

[3] Rodney A. Smolla is the James Gould Cutler Professor of Constitutional Law, and director of the Institute of Bill of Rights Law at the College of William and Mary, Marshall-Wythe School of Law. He received his B.A. from Yale in 1975, and his J.D. from Duke in 1978, where he graduated first in his class, and was Note and Comment editor of the *Duke Law Journal*. After law school he clerked for Judge Charles Clark of the United States Court of Appeals for the Fifth Circuit and practiced law at Mayer, Brown & Platt in Chicago. He has taught at the DePaul, Illinois, Indiana, Arkansas and Denver law schools.

Smolla has published numerous law review articles and is the author of three books. His first book, *Suing the Press: Libel, the Media and Power*, (New York: Oxford University Press, 1986), received the American Bar Association Gavel Award Certificate of Merit in 1987. He is the author of *Law of Defamation*, (New York: Clark, Boardman Publishing Co., 1986) and *Jerry Falwell v. Larry Flynt: The First Amendment on Trial*, (New York: St. Martin's Press, 1988).

[4] *Annenberg Proposal*, *supra* note 1, p. 10.

[5] *Ibid.*, p. 19.

[6] *New York Times Co. v. Sullivan*, 376 U.S. 254 (1964).

[7] Johnston, Harry M., III and Kaufman, Henry R., "Annenberg, *Sullivan* at twenty-five, and the question of libel reform," *Communications Lawyer: A Publication of the Forum on Communications Law*, American Bar Association, Vol. 7, No. 1, Winter 1989, p. 4.

[8] Kierstead, Robert L., "Overhauling the libel system," *Boston Globe*, Nov. 28, 1988.

[9] Sitomer, Curtis Jr., "Libel is *not* having to say you're sorry!", *Christian Science Monitor*, Nov. 10, 1988, p. 23.

[10] "Reforming libel law," *National Law Journal*, Oct. 24, 1988.

[11] Benson Goldberg, Stephanie, "New proposal to deal with libel," *American Bar Association Journal*, Jan. 1989, p. 34.

[12] Leval, Pierre, "The no-money, no-fault libel suit: Keeping *Sullivan* in its proper place," *Harvard Law Review*, Vol. 101, 1988, p. 1287.

[13] Traynor, Michael, "Defamation law: Shock absorbers for its ride into the groves of academe," *Journal of College and University Law*, Vol. 16, No. 3, Winter 1990, p. 373.

[14] *Neary v. Regents of the University of California*, Superior Court of California, Alameda County, No. 525-839-0.

[15] "Defamation law: Shock absorbers for its ride into the groves of academe," *supra* note 13, p. 377, n. 10.

[16] Smolla, Rodney A. and Gaertner, Michael J., "The Annenberg libel reform proposal: The case for enactment," *William and Mary Law Review*, Vol. 31, No. 1, Fall 1989, pp. 25, 64-65.

IV. The Libel Dispute Resolution Program: A Way To Resolve Disputes Out of Court
John Soloski and Roselle L. Wissler

There seems to be a growing consensus among legal scholars, media attorneys, journalists, and judges that current libel law does not serve the interests of the media, plaintiffs, or the public. The high degree of dissatisfaction with the existing libel litigation system has led a number of legal scholars to offer proposals to reform libel law.[1] Bills also have been introduced in Congress and in a number of state legislatures to modify libel law significantly.[2] All of these bills have died in committee and, so far, none of the libel law reform proposals has been implemented.

However, a way of resolving libel disputes that avoids most of the problems of current libel law already exists. The Iowa Libel Research Project has developed and implemented an alternative process for resolving libel disputes outside of the courts called the Libel Dispute Resolution Program. The purpose of this experimental program, which began in 1987, is to test the viability of using a nonlitigation process for resolving libel disputes which involve the media. This essay explains why the program was developed and describes how it works.

The results of the experimental phase of the program will be available in late 1991.

The Real Cost of Libel

For most of its history, libel law favored plaintiffs. Under common law, a plaintiff could win a libel suit by showing that the allegedly libelous statements had injured his or her reputation.[3] For all practical purposes, the falsity of the allegedly libelous statements was presumed, and the burden fell on the publisher to prove that the statements were true. "If publication, defamation (reputational disparagement), and injury could be shown, the publisher was strictly liable, even if there was an honest mistake or understandable oversight."[4] Because money damages were the remedy available to libel plaintiffs, there was a fear that the prospect of having to pay large damages would have a "chilling effect" on the media's willingness to report controversial news stories.

In 1964, the U.S. Supreme Court radically changed libel law and in so doing seemingly provided the news media with enormous protection from libel suits. In *New York Times Co. v. Sullivan*,[5] the Court ruled that public figures had to show that an allegedly libelous statement was published with knowledge of its falsity or with reckless disregard of probable falsity. In *Gertz v. Robert Welch, Inc.*,[6] the Supreme Court extended the news media's protection from libel suits by requiring private plaintiffs to show that the media acted at least negligently when publishing libelous statements. The Supreme Court's purpose in *Sullivan* and *Gertz* was to provide the news media protection from liability for inadvertently publishing false information so as not to fetter the free and robust discussion of issues of public importance.

The actual-malice rule of *Sullivan* and the negligence rule of *Gertz* (also referred to as constitutional privileges) are considered to be major victories for the press. To prevail in a libel suit today, plaintiffs need to show not only that the information published about them is false, but that the media published the information with some degree of negligence, with actual knowledge of its falsity, or with reckless disregard of the truth. It was assumed the constitutional privileges would reduce the danger of the media having to pay large damage awards by making it more difficult for plaintiffs, especially public plaintiffs, to win a libel suit. But despite the substantial hurdles plaintiffs face as a result of the constitutional privileges, they continue to sue the media for libel. As a result, libel remains a serious problem for the media.

The biggest danger the media face in a libel suit is losing and having to pay large damage awards. But this does not happen often. The media lose very few cases[7] and when they do lose, damage awards are often reduced on appeal.[8] The real economic impact of libel on the media is the high cost of defending a seriously litigated suit.[9] To defend such a suit today typically costs a media outlet $150,000 and more if the case is appealed.[10] It has been reported that four-fifths of all the money spent by the media on libel litigation goes to pay legal expenses, mostly attorneys' fees.[11] Even the cost of obtaining the most expeditious outcome of a libel suit is expensive. Garbus reported that by the time a motion for summary judgment is filed, a typical media outlet has already spent $20,000 on legal fees.[12] But because most summary judgment decisions are appealed, the final cost of ending a libel case at the summary judgment stage is about $80,000.[13] The cost of defending some recent celebrated libel suits has been astronomical. CBS spent between $6 and $10 million in defending the Westmoreland case[14] and Time, Inc. spent $1.5 million in the Sharon case.[15]

The major reason for these high defense costs is that libel litigation has become more complex as a result of the constitutional privileges. Because plaintiffs must show the media were at fault, the primary focus of a libel suit is not on the truth or falsity of the alleged libel but on how the media arrived at the disputed story. This means the news media must open their editorial processes to plaintiffs who are in search of evidence necessary to prove fault. Time-consuming and expensive depositions of journalists, examination of journalists' notes and other papers, and exhaustive examination of newsroom procedures are normal parts of libel suits. And this inquiry extends not only to the way journalists performed, but to their state of mind as they did their work.

Ironically, the constitutional privileges, intended to protect freedom of the press, may actually threaten it. By making fault an issue, journalistic performance is what is adjudicated in most libel suits. In the typical libel case, the court must examine how the disputed story was done and decide whether the defendant behaved appropriately.[16] As Judge Pierre N. Leval has pointed out, a libel suit is, in effect, an attack on the journalistic integrity of the news media.[17] It is the cost of defending their journalistic integrity that places such a huge financial burden on the media.[18] The constitutional privileges, intended to protect the media from large damage awards, actually make libel a serious economic threat to the media.

Because of the high cost of defending a libel suit, the fear of suit, despite the media's knowing that a plaintiff is unlikely to prevail, is seen as deterring the media from pursuing or publishing controversial stories of public importance.[19] Plaintiffs interested in punishing the media for publishing truthful but damaging stories can file a libel suit knowing that the media will have to pay large legal fees to defend themselves.[20] These undeserving plaintiffs also can achieve public vindication of their reputation through their libel suit because they are not likely to lose their suit for four or more years, long after the time when most people have forgotten the original story.[21]

Yet another irony of current libel law is that its concern with money damages is largely irrelevant to most libel plaintiffs. In fact, the underlying assumptions of the libel system bear surprisingly little relationship to the objectives of plaintiffs.

Why Plaintiffs Sue

To find out what motivates plaintiffs to sue for libel, the Iowa Libel Research Project interviewed over 160 plaintiffs who had sued the media.[22] One of the major conclusions reached by this study is that plaintiffs are primarily concerned with the underlying falsity of the allegedly libelous statements and with restoring their reputation. According to the plaintiffs, obtaining monetary compensation for damage to their reputation is not their primary objective immediately following the publication of the alleged libel. The Iowa researchers have been criticized as having too readily accepted plaintiffs' claims that they are more interested in restoring their reputations than in winning money damages. But on closer inspection of the data, it is not surprising that plaintiffs are primarily motivated by a desire to repair their reputations.

As a group, plaintiffs are not fly-by-night operators, but are well-established and highly visible members of their communities. Often they are community leaders who hold important elected or appointed positions. The Iowa Libel Research Project's data show that the typical libel plaintiff is an affluent, well-educated, life-long resident of his community, whose employment brings him into almost daily contact with the public. More often than not, the typical libel plaintiff's ability to earn a living is directly related to his public reputation. In addition, most libel plaintiffs are not especially litigious; their libel suit is often the only law suit they have ever filed.

Plaintiff interest in obtaining reputational repair immediately following publication of the alleged libel is not surprising when the type of damage caused by the alleged libel is examined. Very few plaintiffs said that they suffered financial harm as a result of the alleged libel. Most plaintiffs said that they suffered emotional harm or that the alleged libel had damaged their business, professional, or political reputation. Only 14 percent of the plaintiffs said the alleged libel had caused them financial harm, and another 22 percent said that they suffered both emotional and financial harm.

Plaintiff actions immediately following publication of the alleged libel indicate that restoring their reputation is their primary concern. If plaintiffs were primarily interested in obtaining money damages, one would assume that they would immediately contact an attorney with the specific intent of filing a libel suit. However, this is not the case. Nearly 90 percent of the plaintiffs interviewed said that they, on their own, through their attorney, or with their attorney, had contacted the media prior to filing suit in an attempt to resolve the dispute. And 78 percent of these plaintiffs said that the media were asked to run a retraction, correction, or apology. An additional 6 percent of the plaintiffs said that the media were asked to discuss the story with them, and 3 percent said the media were asked to provide space or air time for them to respond to the alleged libel. Nearly 73 percent of the plaintiffs said that they would have been satisfied if the media had run a retraction, correction, or apology immediately after the alleged libel had appeared. In all, less than 4 percent said that they would have been satisfied only if the media had paid them money damages. Interestingly, even those plaintiffs who said the libel caused them financial harm said that they would have been satisfied if the media had retracted or corrected the alleged libel.

Thus, the type of harm caused by the alleged libel, the actions plaintiffs took immediately following publication, and what they asked the media to do about the alleged libel support the Iowa Research Project's finding that plaintiffs are primarily motivated by a desire to repair their reputations. But once the decision to sue is made, the objectives of some plaintiffs undergo a not-unexpected change. Although reputational repair remains the objective of most plaintiffs, about 30 percent of the plaintiffs said they sued in order to punish the media, and about one-fifth said they sued in order to win money damages. The plaintiffs in this last group tended to be those who suffered real economic loss because of the alleged libel. While an immediate correction or retraction of the alleged libel would have mitigated the financial damages suffered by these plaintiffs, by the time suit had been filed, any economic harm caused by the alleged libel could no longer be remedied by correction or retraction alone. Also contributing to the change in plaintiff objectives was the high level of frustration and anger plaintiffs felt toward the media. This resulted not simply from the media's rejection of their request for a retraction, correction, or apology, but also from the way the media treated the plaintiffs following publication. Most plaintiffs said they were angered by their contact with the media following the publication of the alleged libel, and most plaintiffs said that the media's treatment of them was a significant factor in their decision to sue.

Most of the libel plaintiffs interviewed lost their suits. But it would be a mistake to measure plaintiffs' success simply by examining the outcome of their libel suits. Despite losing, plaintiffs said that their suit had achieved important reputational goals. Over 40 percent of the plaintiffs said their libel suit had successfully defended their reputation and another 40 percent reported that it had stopped adverse publicity about them. Remarkably, over 86 percent of the plaintiffs said that they would sue again if faced with a similar situation. The plaintiff most committed to suing is the plaintiff most in the public eye. This is precisely the type of plaintiff current libel law means to discourage from suing. These facts suggest that for these plaintiffs, the very act of suing is a form of self-help, and that plaintiffs use libel suits as a means of publicly vindicating their reputations.

Despite the plaintiffs' feelings that their libel suits had accomplished important reputational goals, and despite their resolve to sue again if faced with a similar situation, plaintiffs expressed a high degree of dissatisfaction with their litigation experience. Over 65 percent of the plaintiffs reported that they were dissatisfied or extremely dissatisfied. And a large number of these plaintiffs directed their dissatisfaction toward the legal system and not the media. This suggests that there is a disjunction between the objectives of plaintiffs and those of the legal system.

One measure of this disjunction is the amount of interest plaintiffs expressed in using a nonlitigation process for resolving the dispute. The proposed process would be prompt, fair, determine the accuracy of the libelous statements, and require publication of the outcome; however, it would provide no money damages. Nearly 70 percent of the plaintiffs said they would seriously consider using such a process, and another 13 percent said they would consider such a process under certain conditions. Only 14 percent of the plaintiffs said they would not consider using a nonlitigation process for resolving the dispute. The features of the process that plaintiffs found most attractive were: (1) having the outcome made public; (2) avoiding suit; (3) achieving a more just outcome; and (4) reducing time and cost.

It is possible that the plaintiffs' interest in a nonlitigation process is a result of hindsight, and that plaintiffs who have never experienced a libel suit would not be equally receptive to using such a process. Nevertheless, plaintiff interest in reputational repair and their actions following publication of the alleged libel suggest that the development of a nonlitigation process—which would focus on the underlying truth or falsity of the alleged libel and would be quick and inexpensive—is worthy of exploration.

The Libel Dispute Resolution Program

The major problems with current libel law can be summarized briefly. The media face lengthy and expensive litigation with the possibility of paying sizeable damage awards if they should lose. In addition, there is a great deal of intrusion into the editorial process because the law requires the media to open their editorial process to court scrutiny. For plaintiffs, the law's concern with fault does not address what plaintiffs say they care most about: the underlying falsity of the alleged libel. And lacking any other way of responding to the alleged libel, plaintiffs resort to the legal system as a means of publicly vindicating their reputations. The disjunction between the goals of libel law and the objectives of plaintiffs, coupled with the ever-present threat of economic loss that libel possesses for the media, suggests that a quicker, cheaper method focusing on truth or falsity would be attractive to both plaintiffs and the media.

To that end, the Iowa Libel Research Project developed the Libel Dispute Resolution Program to implement and evaluate a voluntary process for resolving libel disputes involving the media. The program is being run in cooperation with the American Arbitration Association.

The program is designed to be very flexible, with the parties negotiating most of the specific procedures to be used in the process. One of the primary goals of the program is to open lines of communication between the parties. Already, the program has facilitated settlement of libel disputes by acting as an intermediary between the parties. Appendix 1 outlines the specific procedures of the Libel Dispute Resolution Program. What follows is a description of how the program works.

Either party to a media libel dispute, its counsel, or a judge may ask the Libel Dispute Resolution Program staff to ascertain whether the parties are willing to submit the dispute to the program. The dispute should be one that is likely to be seriously litigated and that involves statements of a factual nature which have damaged the complainant's reputation. The program staff will explain the procedures available and assist the parties in fashioning the process.

During the experimental phase of the Libel Dispute Resolution Program, the staff is dealing primarily with attorneys who represent clients involved in libel disputes. Disputes are being referred by a variety of sources, including a major libel insurer, attorneys, and media personnel. Once the staff has identified a dispute that might be resolved by the program, staff members contact the attorneys for each side to explain the program and to ascertain their interest in using it. One member of the staff is assigned to work with each party's attorney.

After the parties have decided to use the program and have negotiated the details of the process, they complete a submission agreement. In this document, the parties agree to submit the dispute to the Libel Dispute Resolution Program under its rules, to abide by the agreed-upon remedy, and to waive further legal action. The submission agreement also includes a brief statement of the nature of the dispute and the negotiated specifics of the process.

The issues to be adjudicated are the existence of reputational harm and the truth or falsity of the challenged statements. Fault-related issues, such as malice, negligence, and the reasonableness of the editorial process are not relevant, and discovery and evidence relating to such issues are prohibited. The complaining party has the burden of identifying the specific statements that are alleged to be false, has to show that the challenged statements have caused reputational harm, and, unless the parties agree otherwise, has the burden of proving that the statements are false.

The remedy is subject to negotiation, but is likely to consist of the respondent's agreeing to publish or broadcast in full a brief written finding on the falsity issue or to pay to have the finding published or broadcast in other comparable media. The parties, by agreement, may depart from this and determine any other non-monetary remedy. If the parties agree, reasonable attorneys' fees may be awarded to the prevailing party.

The process is strictly scheduled to expedite resolution of the dispute, to minimize any monetary loss experienced by the complainant as a result of the alleged libel. The dispute should be resolved in 60 to 75 days. If the parties choose to proceed directly to a hearing, they may do so. In such cases, they only need to have a telephone conference call with a "neutral" (*i.e.*, arbitrator) before the hearing, in order to resolve any remaining questions or conflicts concerning information to be exchanged or the conduct of the hearing.

Many parties, however, may find a pre-hearing settlement conference to be useful. The goals of the conference include reducing the scope of the dispute, encouraging stipulations of uncontested facts, and encouraging settlement discussions. The settlement conference is private and informal and requires the attendance of the parties as well as counsel. All admissions, proposals, and statements made in the course of the conference are confidential and inadmissible in the hearing or in any other proceeding.

Parties may choose between a settlement conference that involves mediation or one that involves assessment by a special master. The mediator helps the parties analyze their dispute and encourages them to consider how they might be able to reach a mutually satisfactory settlement. The mediator's role is advisory; a mediator cannot make a finding on the dispute. The mediator guides the parties' discussion about relevant information and seeks to devise a formula for settlement. The mediator may offer suggestions and point out things that the parties may have overlooked, helping to clarify issues. The mediator may meet privately with each party to get a clearer understanding of the issues in an attempt to bring the parties' offers closer together. The mediator will work with both sides toward establishing realistic, acceptable claims and offers. Negotiating, with or without the help of a mediator, is voluntary. If a party does not like the way negotiations are progressing, the process can be terminated.

The special master helps the parties identify areas of agreement and assesses their relative positions on areas of disagreement. The special master cannot make a finding on the dispute. The special master will note areas of disagreement, probing support for differing views of the facts. The special master assesses the relative strengths and weaknesses of each side's evidence and arguments on key issues. If the parties are interested, the special master will help them explore settlement options. If the parties are not interested in discussing settlement, or if they try but fail to reach a settlement, the special master will offer an assessment of how the dispute would likely be resolved at a hearing, and why.

For those disputes that have not reached a settlement, the dispute will be submitted to a hearing before a neutral. The hearing is public unless both parties agree that it should be closed. The parties, by mutual agreement, control the range of issues to be resolved, the scope of the remedy, and many of the procedural aspects of the hearing process. Usually, the complainant presents his or her case first, followed by the respondent. Hearings are conducted by the neutral in a manner that permits a fair presentation of the case by both parties. The hearing is less formal than a court trial, and neutrals are not required to follow strict rules of evidence. The neutral decides which evidence offered by the parties is relevant to the dispute and can reject any evidence they submit.

The hearing is ended only after both parties have had full opportunity to present their cases. The neutral will issue a brief written finding within 10 days. The neutral's finding will state the factual questions at issue; the existence of reputational harm; the truth, falsity, or indeterminacy of the facts as found; and the basis upon which the finding has been made.

The neutrals selected for this program are drawn from a specifically compiled panel of experienced neutrals provided by the American Arbitration Association. The panel consists mainly of retired judges and senior attorneys who average 15 years experience as neutrals. The neutrals for the settlement conference are appointed by the American Arbitration Association. The parties select the neutral to conduct the hearing. The parties will be provided with information on the neutrals and must advise the American Arbitration Association of any objections. Any personal, professional, or business contacts between the parties and the neutrals must be declared. If there is a disclosure of a disqualifying nature, the neutral will be replaced.

The Benefits of Resolving Libel Disputes Out of Court

The case of *Kadet v. Daytona (Fla.) Times*[23] illustrates the benefits of an out-of-court alternative for resolving libel disputes. The case had been in litigation for three and one-half years at an estimated cost of $100,000 in donated legal fees to the newspaper defendant. In 1987, the parties agreed to dismiss the suit and submit it to a six-person panel which was to determine the truth or falsity of the alleged libel. The panel could not award any damages.

The panel found unanimously that the alleged libel was false, but that the paper had accurately reported the statements of a second defendant. The panel split as to whether the statements were published with malice and whether the plaintiff's reputation had been damaged. The plaintiff was pleased with the finding on falsity and with the paper's publication of the finding. The paper also was pleased with the outcome because of the time and money saved.

This case illustrates the success of an alternative process that was created specifically for this dispute. The Libel Dispute Resolution Program should result in an even more efficient and satisfactory resolution of libel disputes because it can be initiated earlier in the dispute and because it is designed to be more attuned to the goals and interests of the parties.

For plaintiffs, the program provides a quick finding on the falsity question. And because plaintiffs do not need to prove negligence or malice, they will increase their chances of winning on the falsity issue. The publicity generated by the hearing and the likelihood that the respondent will publish the neutral's finding (or pay to have it published elsewhere) will vindicate the plaintiff's reputation.

For the media, the program should substantially reduce the cost of resolving libel disputes. Because there are no money damages at stake, the media are protected from the economic loss that would result should they lose a libel suit in court. This should help to eliminate the "chilling effect" associated with current libel law. In addition, there will be no intrusion into the media's editorial process because fault is not an issue to be decided by the program. This will reduce the media's legal expenses and time involved in having to defend their journalistic procedures.

Benefits of the Program

Not all plaintiffs will be interested in using the Libel Dispute Resolution Program. Plaintiffs who need money to compensate for economic harm caused by the alleged libel will not find the program's non-monetary remedy very attractive. For these plaintiffs, nothing short of obtaining money damages will be satisfactory. But the Iowa Libel Research Project's data show that very few plaintiffs suffer real economic loss because of the alleged libel. The primary concern of most plaintiffs immediately following publication of the alleged libel is the restoration of their damaged reputations. It is these plaintiffs who should find the program appealing.

A pragmatic examination of libel law should lead many plaintiffs and their attorneys to conclude that the Libel Dispute Resolution Program offers a forum for resolving their libel disputes that is better than the legal system. Because of the constitutional privileges, libel law today is not an effective means for achieving reputational repair. Even if a plaintiff can prove that the alleged libel is false, the plaintiff will not win the suit unless fault can be shown. And even if the plaintiff can show fault, the suit is not likely to be resolved for four or more years, long after the time it can effectively repair the plaintiff's reputation. Plaintiffs who are interested in restoring their reputations and in mitigating damages caused by the alleged libel are better off using the Libel Dispute Resolution Program than they are in filing suit. This is especially true for public plaintiffs who bear the heaviest burden under current libel law. And if the parties agree that reasonable attorneys' fees be awarded to the prevailing party, the program offers plaintiffs a way of repairing their reputation without serious economic risk.

But the Iowa Libel Research Project's data also indicate that the time period in which plaintiffs would be most interested in using the program is limited. Plaintiff interest in obtaining a non-monetary resolution of a dispute is highest immediately following publication of the alleged libel. Consequently, the time period in which the Libel Dispute Resolution Program is likely to be most appealing to plaintiffs is within a few days or weeks after publication. Thus, it is in the media's interest to recommend the program at the outset of the dispute. As time passes, it may become increasingly difficult to convince plaintiffs to use the program.

In addition to eliminating money damages from the libel equation, the Libel Dispute Resolution Program provides the media with other important safeguards. In the program, the burden of proof falls mostly on the plaintiff. The plaintiff must identify the specific statements that are alleged to be false and must prove that the statements damaged his or her reputation. And unless the parties agree otherwise, the plaintiff bears the burden of proving that the allegedly libelous statements are false. Also, what is to be determined in the program is not the literal truth of the disputed statements but, rather, whether the statements are substantially true. As long as the gist of the story is true, the media should prevail in the hearing. Minor factual errors that cannot be shown to have damaged a plaintiff's reputation are not an issue to be decided by the program. By requiring a plaintiff to show that the alleged libel caused reputational damage, the program should discourage suits by those who want to use the program to correct minor factual errors in stories about them.

Any program that provides a way of resolving libel disputes outside of the courts will be the subject of criticism. Some critics of the Libel Dispute Resolution Program, many of whom are members of the media defense bar, have suggested that establishing the underlying truth or falsity of the alleged libel is such a difficult task that there will be no significant savings in litigation costs for the media. This criticism, however, is premature. It is not possible to predict how difficult it will be to determine the truth or falsity of the alleged libel until after the Libel Dispute Resolution Program has been in use for a number of years.[24] And it also should be pointed out that unless the parties agree otherwise, it is the plaintiff who bears the burden of proving that the allegedly libelous statements are false. Furthermore, establishing the underlying truth or falsity of the alleged libel should be as much in the interest of the media as of plaintiffs because, after all, the media are not in the misinformation business.

Critics have also suggested that the Libel Dispute Resolution Program will increase the number of libel actions filed against the media and, likewise, will not reduce the media's legal costs. But again, this cannot be said with any certainty until the program has been in regular use for a number of years. It should be noted, however, that the program is voluntary and the media need not use it for every dispute. Without the consent of the media, plaintiffs cannot, on their own, elect to use the program. Frivolous libel suits should be discouraged because the media can choose to defend such suits in the courts. And a plaintiff who is the subject of a damaging, yet truthful, story should be discouraged by the risk that the truth of the story will be confirmed by the neutral. And even if the media must defend more actions, it is likely that the total cost would be much lower than the media's current legal bills for defending suits in the courts.

Conclusion

Because the Libel Dispute Resolution Program is voluntary, it possesses one key advantage: It allows the media to keep their hard-won constitutional privileges for those cases best dealt with by the courts, while providing an alternative forum for resolving libel disputes in which establishing the truth of the alleged libel is of utmost concern to the parties. Similarly, plaintiffs who need money damages to repair the harm caused by the alleged libel are not precluded from seeking such damages in the courts. This is in direct contrast to the Annenberg proposal in which a plaintiff can sue for money only if the media defendant elects not to use the declaratory judgment option.[25] But for the majority of plaintiffs who are interested in repairing their reputations, the Libel Dispute Resolution Program offers a better and quicker way of achieving this than does the legal system.

The Libel Dispute Resolution Program is experimental. After four years, the results of the program will be analyzed and published. The program will continue, however, regardless of whether it has been able to resolve any significant number of libel disputes. The American

Arbitration Association has agreed to administer the Libel Dispute Resolution Program after the Iowa Libel Research Project completes its study, thereby assuring that at least one alternative method of resolving conflicts will remain available to the public.

Notes

[1] E.g., *Proposal for the Reform of Libel Law: The Report of the Libel Reform Project of The Annenberg Washington Program*, (Washington: The Annenberg Washington Program in Communications Policy Studies of Northwestern University, 1988) [hereinafter cited as *Annenberg Proposal*]; Barrett, "Declaratory judgments for libel: A better alternative," *California Law Review*, Vol. 74, 1986, p. 847; and Franklin, "A declaratory judgment alternative to current libel law," *California Law Review*, Vol. 74, 1986, p. 809.

[2] H.R. 2846, 99th Congress, 1st Session (1985). Among the states in which bills have been introduced to modify libel law are Illinois (H.B. 590, Ill. Leg. 85th Cong.); Iowa (Senate File 40); Connecticut (H.B. 5932, Conn. Leg.); and California (S. 1979 Cal. Leg., Reg. Sess.).

[3] Bezanson, R., Cranberg, G., and Soloski, J., *Libel Law and the Press: Myth and Reality*, (New York: The Free Press, 1987), p. 1 [hereinafter cited as *Libel Law and the Press*]. See also Bezanson, "The libel tort today," *Washington and Lee Law Review*, Vol. 45, 1988, p. 353; and Bezanson and Murchison, "The three voices of libel," *Washington and Lee Law Review*, Vol. 47, 1990, p. 213.

[4] *Ibid.*

[5] *New York Times Co. v. Sullivan*, 376 U.S. 254 (1964).

[6] *Gertz v. Robert Welch, Inc.*, 418 U.S. 323 (1974).

[7] *Libel Law and the Press*, supra note 3, p. 112.

[8] Levine and Perry reported that the largest damage award ever affirmed by the U.S. Supreme Court in a libel case was for $3 million. (Levine and Perry, "No way to celebrate the Bill of Rights: Punitive damage awards go through the ceiling," *Columbia Journalism Review*, Vol. 29, No. 2, July-Aug. 1990, p. 39.) In an editor's note that accompanied this article, *Columbia Journalism Review* reported that the two largest damage awards ever entered against the media were for $34 million and $31.5 million. The cases that generated these awards are on appeal.

Levine and Perry are concerned that a large number of media libel cases result in the awarding of punitive damages. This is not surprising and it is a direct result of the constitutional privileges. When a plaintiff is able to prove that the media published the libel with actual knowledge of its falsity or with reckless disregard of the truth, the jury often awards punitive damages in order to penalize the media for what amounts to "journalistic malpractice."

100 BEYOND THE COURTROOM

[9] Libel insurance premiums have leveled off in the last few years as a result of a decrease in the number of libel suits being filed. However, in the mid-1980s, libel insurance premiums increased by 50 to 100 percent annually. Also, insurance companies have established co-insurance, which requires clients to pay a percentage of all legal fees above a deductible. *See* Newsom, "Decline in libel activity prompts insurance rate 'stability,'" *Presstime*, Vol. 9, Nov. 1987, p. 38; Newsom, "Newspapers adjust budgets as premiums rise," *Presstime*, Vol. 8, April 1986, p. 8; and Massing, "Libel insurance: Scrambling for coverage," *Columbia Journalism Review*, Vol. 24, Jan.-Feb. 1986, p. 36.

[10] Genovese, "Libel update: Issues remain heated in legislatures, courtrooms," *Presstime*, Vol. 8, April 1986, p. 37. *See also* Garbus, "The many costs of libel," *Publishers Weekly*, Vol. 230, Sept. 5, 1986, p. 34. Adding to the cost of litigation is the media's unwillingness to settle libel suits. It is difficult to obtain specific information about rates of settlement, but indications are that between 10 and 20 percent of media libel cases are settled. This settlement rate is far below that for other civil disputes in which nearly 90 percent are successfully settled by attorneys. *See Libel Law and the Press*, *supra* note 3, p. 145; and Trubek, D., Grossman, J., Felstiner, W., Kritzer, H., and Surat, A., "Civil litigation research project final report," unpublished, University of Wisconsin Law School, Madison, Wis., 1983. One reason for the media's reluctance to settle libel suits is a concern that settling cases will result in more libel suits being filed.

[11] "The many costs of libel," *supra* note 10.

[12] *Ibid*.

[13] "Libel update: Issues remain heated in legislatures, courtrooms," *supra* note 10.

[14] Goodale, "Survey of recent media verdicts, their disposition on appeal, and media defense costs," *Media Insurance and Risk Management 1985*, (New York: Practicing Law Institute, 1985), pp. 69, 87.

[15] Kaplan, "The judge's postmortem of the Sharon trial," *National Law Journal*, March 8, 1985, p. 27. The Sharon case is noteworthy because Judge Abraham Sofaer instructed the jury to reach a separate verdict on whether the allegedly libelous statements were false, whether the statements defamed the plaintiff, and whether the defendant acted with malice. The jury found the statements were false and that they had defamed the plaintiff, but found that the defendant had not acted with malice. Even though *Time* won the case, it was widely perceived that Sharon had prevailed on the issues most important to him and that the verdict had vindicated his reputation.

[16] Cranberg, "Searching for 'fault'...Libel judges are setting standards for the press," *Washington Journalism Review*, Vol. 11, No. 7, Sept. 1989, p. 42. The Iowa

THE LIBEL DISPUTE RESOLUTION PROGRAM   101

Libel Research Project is in the midst of a detailed examination of court-created journalistic standards. The results of this study should be available in late 1991.

[17] Leval, "The no-money, no-fault libel suit: Keeping *Sullivan* in its proper place," *Harvard Law Review*, Vol. 101, 1988, p. 1287.

[18] Leval, who presided at the trial of General Westmoreland's libel suit against CBS, wrote that in *Westmoreland*, "the *Sullivan* discovery included detailed depositions of fifteen reporters, researchers, editors, and production personnel who participated in making the CBS documentary, as well as several of the program's sources to inquire whether they had been influenced in their answers." *Ibid.*, p. 1295.

[19] Massing, "The libel chill: How cold is it out there?", *Columbia Journalism Review*, Vol. 24, May-June 1985, p. 31.

[20] Libel suits have been used to stifle private individuals' political expression. *See* Canan and Pring, "Strategic lawsuits against public participation," *Social Problems*, Vol. 35, Dec. 1988, p. 506.

[21] "Declaratory judgments for libel: A better alternative," *supra* note 1.

[22] The empirical findings discussed in this section come from *Libel Law and the Press*, *supra* note 3.

[23] "Libel dispute ended by stipulation for expert panel resolution," *Alternative Dispute Resolution Report*, Vol. 1, April 30, 1987, p. 5.

[24] Smolla and Gaertner have pointed out that it is not possible to design any system for dealing with libel that "does not include truth or falsity as an issue for litigation. . . .[because] [a]t the base libel is a lie." (Smolla and Gaertner, "The Annenberg libel reform proposal: The case for enactment," *William and Mary Law Review*, Vol. 31, No. 1, Fall 1989, pp. 25, 55.)

The Annenberg proposal also has been criticized for placing the truth or falsity of the alleged libel at the heart of its process. But Smolla and Gaertner point out that the "'truth' attacks can be misleading because they are often attacks not really aimed at the Annenberg proposal's method of litigating truth, but rather at the possibility of liability without fault as part of the proposal's declaratory judgment scheme. The sore point is not so much truth, as liability without fault."

Some critics fear that the Annenberg proposal, if adopted, would have a chilling effect on journalists because a journalist's reputation would be damaged if the alleged libel is shown to be false. (*Ibid.*, p. 54.)

[25] *Annenberg Proposal*, *supra* note 1.

Appendix 1
Libel Dispute Resolution Program Procedures

1. Eligibility Criteria

1.1 The dispute should be one which is expected to be seriously litigated.
1.2 Disputes will not be eligible for consideration if they are determined by the Libel Dispute Resolution Program (hereinafter referred to as the Program) to involve (a) challenged statements of a nonfactual nature or (b) the absence of reputational harm.
1.3 For research purposes, the parties and attorneys must be willing to be interviewed and to have the proceedings observed and recorded by the Program. All information collected for research purposes shall be strictly confidential and the parties will remain anonymous. The research will be reported in such a way that the parties will not be identifiable.

2. Issues To Be Adjudicated

2.1 The complainant shall have the burden of defining the specific published/broadcast statements that are alleged to be false, must show that the challenged statements have caused reputational harm, and, unless the parties agree otherwise, shall have the burden of proof of the issue of falsity.
2.2 The issues to be adjudicated shall be (a) the existence of reputational harm and (b) the truth or falsity of alleged and defined factual statements or assertions published/broadcast by the responding publisher/broadcaster. Whether the challenged statement is one of fact will be determined by the words published or inferences reasonably implied by the publication, even though not expressed explicitly in the text.
2.3 In cases where the publisher republished information alleged to be false, every effort should be made to have the original source

included as a party to the proceeding. Regardless of whether the source's inclusion is possible, the issue to be adjudicated shall be the truth or falsity of the underlying facts. The finding may also indicate (a) that the respondent had obtained the information from another party who was unwilling to cooperate in the proceedings; or (b) whether the respondent had accurately reported what the source had said.

2.4 The finding will contain a statement that no determination of the publisher's/broadcaster's fault or the reasonableness of its procedures has been made, nor should such a conclusion be drawn from the finding.

3. Remedy

3.1 If the neutral decides that the dispute involves factual statements and that reputational harm has occurred, the neutral shall make a written finding on the falsity issue. If the neutral decides that no reputational harm has occurred, the neutral's written finding shall so state and the falsity issue need not be addressed.

3.2 The finding of the neutral shall be available for publication.

3.3 The respondent shall agree to publish/broadcast the neutral's finding in full or, in lieu of such agreement, shall agree to pay the other party to have the findings published/broadcast by the respondent or in other comparable media such that the finding is likely to reach the same audience as the original publication/broadcast. The specifics of the remedy shall be subject to the negotiation of the parties.

3.4 The parties, by agreement, may depart from the remedy outlined in Section 3.3 and determine any other non-monetary remedy.

3.5 Attorneys' fees may be available on terms agreed to by the parties.

4. Submission Agreement To Initiate Process

In order to initiate the process, parties must file a signed copy of a written submission agreement to proceed under these rules. It shall include the following points.

4.1 The parties agree to submit the dispute to this alternative process under its rules. The rules shall be effective unless the parties have specified otherwise. The rules will be supplemented by the Mediation and Arbitration Rules of the American Arbitration Association (hereinafter referred to as the administrator).

4.2 The parties agree to abide by the agreed-upon remedy and to waive any further legal action.

4.3 In the absence of an agreement otherwise, each party agrees that it shall bear the cost it incurs in connection with preparation for the proceedings (*e.g.*, legal costs and fees, travel, photocopying, and witnesses).

4.4 The parties agree that neither the Program, the administrator, nor the neutrals shall be liable to any party for any act or omission in connection with any action under the rules.

4.5 The Program, the administrator, and the neutrals shall not divulge any information produced in these proceedings and shall not testify in regard to the dispute in any adversary proceedings or judicial forum.

4.6 The submission agreement shall include the names, addresses, and phone numbers of all parties, their representatives and counsel, and a brief statement of the nature of the dispute, including the specific factual statements that are alleged to be false, or the procedure by which they are to be determined.

4.7 The parties shall determine the elements of the process which are negotiable (remedy, information exchange, type of settlement conference, formality of the hearing, location of the hearing, etc.) within the general parameters of the alternative process.

5. Scheduling

5.1 Schedule:
Day (on or before)
1 sign submission agreement
7 neutrals selected/appointed
21 information exchange
30 settlement conference
50 hearing
60 receive finding

5.2 The parties may agree to change these times, but the schedule they establish should ensure that the dispute will be resolved within 75 calendar days.

5.3 The administrator will help the parties set a date and time for the exchange, conference, and hearing that is convenient for both parties and the neutral.

5.4 Any request to extend an agreed-upon deadline must be presented to the administrator and may be granted only for good cause.

6. Selection of the Neutrals

6.1 Immediately after the filing of the submission agreement, each party simultaneously will be given an identical list of five neutrals from which one neutral shall be appointed to conduct the hearing. Each party shall have the right to strike two names from the list on a preemptory basis and an unlimited number with cause. If the list is not returned within seven days, all persons named therein shall be deemed acceptable. From among the persons who have been approved on both lists, the administrator shall appoint a neutral. The parties shall be given notice by telephone of the appointment of the neutral.

6.2 The administrator shall appoint the neutral for the settlement conference.

6.3 Each party is responsible for promptly (within seven days) disclosing to the administrator and to the other party any circumstances known which would cause reasonable doubt regarding the impartiality of any individual appointed.

6.4 The neutrals shall disclose to the administrator any circumstances likely to affect impartiality, including any bias or any financial or personal interest in the result of the process or any past or present relationship with the parties or their counsel. Upon showing of cause, the administrator will determine whether the neutral shall be disqualified and replaced.

6.5 Administrative and settlement matters will not be heard by the same person selected to conduct the hearing, unless the parties agree otherwise.

6.6 The neutrals shall follow their respective codes of ethics.

6.7 There shall be no *ex parte* communication between the parties and the neutrals other than at the proceedings. Any oral or written communications from the parties to the neutrals shall be directed through the administrator.

7. *Information Exchange*

7.1 In lieu of discovery, there shall be a structured exchange of information (either by meeting or by conference call; if desired, in the presence of a neutral). If both parties agree that a more formal process is needed, they shall agree on a plan for strictly necessary, limited, expeditious discovery aimed at determining the essential facts.

7.2 Any conferences needed to resolve or clarify informational issues will be held by telephone conference call between the attorneys and the administrator or neutral. These conferences will be of an informal nature.

7.3 The information to be exchanged is subject to agreement of the parties, but may include:
   a. the identification of witnesses and a summary of the testimony they are expected to give;
   b. a description of any physical evidence;
   c. copies of documents;

d. summary statements of claims or defenses and the facts underlying them; and

e. offers of admission and stipulation.

7.4 The neutral, during the hearing, shall have the authority to limit information that was not presented during the information exchange.

8. *Settlement Conference*

8.1 The parties shall choose (a) to participate in a settlement conference with either a mediator or a special master (see Sections 8.A and 8.B), or (b) to proceed directly to a hearing. If the parties cannot agree, the Program will assign them randomly to either the mediation or special master conference.

8.2 The goals of the settlement conference include (a) reducing the scope of the dispute by defining and simplifying the issues and by identifying and stipulating to uncontested facts, and (b) encouraging settlement discussions.

8.3 Parties who choose to go directly to a hearing will hold a telephone conference call in order to resolve any remaining questions or conflicts concerning information needed for the hearing.

8.A. Mediation

A.1 The mediator may, but need not, request that the parties submit, a week before the conference, a brief statement that identifies any issues whose resolution might reduce the scope of the dispute or contribute significantly to the productivity of settlement discussions, and their position on these issues.

A.2 The mediation session shall be private and informal.

A.3 The parties as well as counsel must be present during the mediation.

A.4 The mediator does not have authority to impose a settlement upon the parties but will attempt to help them reach a satisfactory resolution of their dispute.

A.5 The mediator is authorized to conduct joint and separate meetings with the parties and to make oral and written recommendations for settlement.

A.6 The mediator is authorized to end the mediation whenever, in the judgment of the mediator, further efforts at mediation would not contribute to a resolution of the dispute between the parties.

A.7 Confidential information disclosed to a mediator by the parties or by witnesses in the course of the mediation shall not be divulged by the mediator.

A.8 The parties shall not rely on or introduce as evidence in any other proceedings, any and all aspects of the mediation effort, including, but not limited to: (a) views expressed or suggestions made by the other party with respect to a possible settlement of the dispute; (b) admissions made by the other party in the course of the mediation proceedings; (c) proposals made or views expressed by the mediator; and (d) the fact that the other party had or had not indicated a willingness to accept a proposal for settlement made by the mediator.

A.9 The mediator shall be disqualified as a hearing or trial witness, consultant, or expert for any party in pending or future action relating to the subject matter of the mediation, including those between persons not parties to the mediation.

8.B. *Special Master*

B.1 The special master may, but need not, request that the parties submit, a week before the conference, a brief statement that identifies any issues whose resolution might reduce the scope of the dispute or contribute significantly to the productivity of settlement discussions, and their position on these issues.

B.2 The conference shall be private and informal.

B.3 The parties as well as counsel should be present at the conference unless otherwise agreed to in advance.

B.4 Each attorney will make a brief presentation of his or her side of the case (focusing on the apparently disputed areas), explaining his or her view of the facts and describing the supporting evidence.

B.5 The special master will identify areas of substantial agreement and encourage stipulations. He or she also will note areas of disagreement, probing the support for differing views of the facts. The special master then will offer his or her assessment of the relative strengths and weaknesses of key evidence and arguments.

B.6 If the parties and counsel are interested, the special master will help them explore settlement options.

B.7 If the parties have no interest in exploring settlement, or if they try but fail to reach an agreement, the special master will provide them with an evaluation of the likely outcome in a hearing and the reasoning behind it.

B.8 All offers, promises, conduct, and statements, whether oral or written, made in the course of the settlement conference by any of the parties, their witnesses or attorneys, or by the special master are confidential and are inadmissible and not discoverable for any purpose in the hearing or in any other litigation.

B.9 The special master shall be disqualified as a hearing or trial witness, consultant, or expert for any party in any pending or future action relating to the subject matter of the settlement conference, including those between persons not parties to the conference.

9. *Hearing*

9.1 The neutral may, but need not, request that the parties submit a brief pre-hearing memo seven to 10 days before the hearing in order to familiarize the neutral with the facts and issues in dispute.

9.2 The hearing shall be public unless both parties agree that it shall be closed. The hearing shall be informal.

9.3 The neutral shall require witnesses to testify under oath.

9.4 Starting with the complainant, each party shall present its claims and proofs and witnesses, who shall submit to questions or other examination. The neutral has discretion to vary this procedure but shall afford full and equal opportunity to all parties for the presentation of any material or relevant proofs.

9.5 The neutral shall be the judge of the relevance and materiality of the evidence offered and conformity to legal rules of evidence shall not be necessary. (The Federal Rules of Evidence may be used as a guide in determining the admissibility of evidence.) Except as probative on the question of truth or falsity, the neutral may rule that evidence relating to procedures, decisions, discussions, documents, or any other materials relating to the reasonableness of publication/broadcast decisions, or fault of the publisher/broadcaster shall neither be admissible nor relevant.

9.6 The parties shall produce such additional evidence as the neutral may deem necessary for an understanding and determination of the dispute. The neutral, when authorized by law to subpoena witnesses or documents, may do so upon the neutral's own initiative or upon the request of any party. All evidence shall be taken in the presence of all the parties, except where any of the parties is absent in default or has waived the right to be present.

9.7 The proceedings shall be recorded for research purposes; the parties may obtain a copy of the recording of the hearing if they wish.

9.8 The neutral shall be empowered to take whatever steps seem appropriate for noncompliance with the procedures.

9.9 If a party fails to present or fails to obtain an adjournment, after due notice, that party shall be declared in default and a finding may be made. The finding of the neutral would include an indication that the party had failed to appear to present or respond to the claim.

9.10 The failure of a witness to appear when requested may, if appropriate, be considered by the neutral in reaching a finding.

9.11 To end the hearing, the neutral shall inquire of all parties whether they have any further proofs to offer or witnesses to be heard; if not, the neutral shall declare the hearing ended.

9.12 The neutral shall make a finding within 10 days of the close of the hearing.

9.13 The written findings of the neutral shall be concise but of sufficient detail to identify the factual question(s) at issue; the existence of reputational harm; the truth, falsity, or indeterminacy of the facts as found; and the basis upon which the finding has been made. The neutral's finding shall also indicate, if the statement is found to be false, the time within which the publisher/broadcaster must comply with the agreed-upon remedy.

V. Alternative Routes to Conflict Resolution: Is This Trip Necessary?

David Bartlett

"Every abuse ought to be reformed, unless the reform is more dangerous than the abuse itself."
—*Voltaire*

"The spirit of improvement is not always a spirit of liberty."
—*John Stuart Mill*

"I'm not really bad. I'm just drawn that way."
—*Jessica Rabbit*

A former commander of American troops in Vietnam files a multi-million-dollar libel suit against CBS. The head of a major international oil company wins a multi-million-dollar libel judgment against the *Washington Post*. The domestic politics of a foreign power and the editorial judgment of an American news magazine collide in a federal courtroom.

Stories like these make bold headlines, but do they represent serious threats to the news media? Do a few big-money libel suits, whatever their final outcome, suggest that freedom of the press is in peril? Is responsible journalism chilled by the current state of libel law? Or does the threat of expensive litigation and gigantic punitive damage awards effectively hold irresponsible journalism in check?

If, as critics from both sides contend, the way we now deal with disputes about news coverage is ineffective and often unfair, is it possible to find practical alternatives? Would these alternatives answer the complaints of those in the news media who claim that the looming threat of enormous libel suits violates their First Amendment rights, and complaints from the public who say that recent judicial interpretations of the First Amendment have unfairly tipped the scales of justice in favor of those who report the news and against those about whom they report?

While some say the present state of libel law unnecessarily inhibits the news media, others argue that the high cost and high risk of libel litigation has an equally chilling effect on potential plaintiffs. By some estimates, up to 90 percent of all libel suits are either dropped or dismissed before trial. One study found that even in cases where the plaintiff wins the first round, the damages he eventually receives after appeal amount to less than 10 percent of what was originally awarded at trial.[1] Not surprisingly, with both sides so unhappy with the present system, a number of alternative approaches to the resolution of conflicts over news coverage have been proposed. They fall into three general categories: new libel laws, arbitration systems, and news councils.

Most of these alternative systems of conflict resolution are theoretically workable, but the larger question of their fairness, constitutionality, and practicality requires careful consideration.

Disputes over press coverage are of two general types: complaints about how journalists go about gathering their material, and disagreements about the accuracy of the news reports they ultimately produce. Invasion of privacy, improper use of sources, misleading reporting tactics, even breaches of simple good taste and manners usually fall into the first category. Libel law deals with the second. Even in the existing system there are numerous ways of dealing with disputes between the news media and those they cover, short of going to court. Letters to the editor, corrections and retractions, follow-up stories, in-house critics, and ombudsmen have all proved effective in settling even serious disputes.

Even those who are most critical of the news media would agree that the press plays a vital role in a free society. The men who wrote the U.S. Constitution recognized from the beginning that effective self-government would depend on a free flow of ideas and information. As society grows larger and more complicated, the importance of the news media (especially radio and television) as agents of this continuous exchange of ideas and information increases accordingly.

The First Amendment grants the news media certain very important privileges. It recognizes the inevitable conflict between the public's right to know and an individual's desire to defend his reputation. For two centuries judges have tried to balance the journalist's right to find and report the news against the ordinary citizen's right to protect his good name. Especially where political debate or criticism of government officials is involved, judges increasingly have come down on the side of journalistic freedom. The free-press provisions of the First Amendment demand that any scheme to reform the way disputes about news coverage are settled allow journalists the widest possible latitude in gathering and reporting the news and commenting on the issues of the day. Any proposal to substitute an alternative method of conflict resolution for the system already in place, therefore, must pass both the test of practicality and the test of constitutionality.

Even before the Revolution, the notion of truth as an absolute defense in libel had taken hold in America. The framers of the Constitution firmly established the sovereignty of the people over their government, and the First Amendment gave this idea practical application by assuring every citizen's right to speak his mind and criticize his government representatives. Except for the short-lived Sedition Act of 1798, which expired before it could be tested in the Supreme Court, the American legal system has never condoned criminal prosecution for criticism of the government.

For a century and a half following ratification of the Constitution, libel law in America remained largely a matter for the states. Only rarely did libel cases reach the Supreme Court, and the legal precedents governing disputes between journalists and those they wrote about evolved piecemeal. It was not until 1925, in fact, that the Supreme

Court got around to ruling that the First Amendment's free-press guarantees applied to the states, and then only in an offhand way.[2] Throughout the 19th century, as the American nation grew in size and complexity, the news media also grew in power and sophistication; their importance as the means by which ordinary citizens were able to inform themselves about government and society grew as well. With rare exceptions, the level of press responsibility and professionalism also improved, at least in comparison to the freewheeling and often viciously partisan style that was accepted as the norm at the time the Constitution and the Bill of Rights were ratified.

While a few jurists, notably Supreme Court Justice Hugo Black, stubbornly held to the absolutist view that the First Amendment means precisely that "Congress shall make no law" in any way abridging freedom of the press,[3] even in cases of deliberate falsehood, it was not until 1964 that the Court chose to lay down a national libel standard that specified what tests a journalist would have to meet in order to enjoy First Amendment protection.[4] Interestingly, the landmark Sullivan case in which the Court addressed this all-important journalistic issue did not deal with a news story at all. Sullivan was an Alabama sheriff who claimed he had been libeled by an advertisement placed in the *New York Times* by a civil-rights group. The advertisement did contain a number of factual errors, and Sullivan was awarded $500,000 in damages by the state courts. But the Supreme Court overturned the verdict on the grounds that threats of large damage awards inhibited reporting on the activities of public officials.

The Sullivan decision established the "actual malice" test as a national libel standard. Henceforth, in order to win a libel suit, a government official would have to prove not only that a news report was false, but also that the news organization either knew it to be untrue or didn't bother to check it out. In other words, the news organization had to be both wrong and at fault. By introducing this notion of fault into libel law, the Court placed the burden of proof in libel cases squarely on the plaintiff's shoulders. But, by requiring the plaintiff to prove not only that a report was false but also that the news organization had not paid sufficient attention to the question of truth or falsity, the Court also made a journalist's motives, procedures, and even his state of mind very much a part of libel litigation for the first time.

The actual-malice standard set forth in the Sullivan decision gives a journalist that all-important "breathing space" he needs to do his job. It grants him the "right to be wrong," as long as his errors are not malicious. At the same time, however, it allows and even encourages what many have come to believe is unwarranted and inhibiting intrusion into the editorial process.

The Sullivan case also serves as an interesting example of the Supreme Court's responsiveness to public opinion. Cynics have always claimed that the Court "reads the election returns," and cases like Sullivan do, in fact, demonstrate that the Court's rulings reflect the ebb and flow of public opinion and the slow but steady development of a national political consensus on important issues. Consider, for example, how the Sullivan case might have been decided by the nine justices who made up the Court in 1934 instead of those sitting in 1964. Or, considering the social climate of the country in 1964, how the Court might have ruled if the advertisement in question had been placed by a segregationist group in order to criticize a government official supportive of the civil-rights struggle.

Unless judges start reading the First Amendment as strictly as Justice Black would have liked, the pendulum of judicial interpretation in matters relating to the news media will always swing back and forth, but at least the courts offer a forum that is reasonably free of the momentary political passion of an elected legislature. Journalists should count themselves lucky to have their fate in the hands of tenured judges rather than elected legislators, even if those judges are occasionally tempted to read the election returns.

Unfortunately for both plaintiffs and news media defendants, the libel cases that followed the landmark Sullivan ruling revealed that fault is no easier to prove than absolute truth. The new obstacles that the Sullivan ruling required plaintiffs to surmount made it much harder for libel judgments to survive the appeals process. The creation of a new class of "public figures" made it much more difficult for plaintiffs to sidestep the actual-malice test. Yet, even as the boundaries of First Amendment protection were extended, the danger to journalism posed by libel suits appeared to increase.

The early 1980s saw Bob Guccione of *Penthouse* Magazine win $40 million in a suit against *Hustler* Magazine. William Tavoulareas of Mobil Oil was awarded more than $2 million in a suit against the *Washington Post*. General William Westmoreland sued CBS News for $120 million. Israeli cabinet minister Ariel Sharon sued *Time* Magazine for $50 million. The Guccione and Tavoulareas verdicts eventually were overturned on appeal. Westmoreland dropped his case before it went to the jury. Sharon went away with a hollow vindication of his claims but received no damages. Nevertheless, for the news media defendant in a major libel case, even costs of a successful defense can be staggering. By some estimates, CBS spent more than $6 million defending the Westmoreland case. On the other hand, of course, the contributors who backed Westmoreland's effort reportedly put up as much as $4 million. It had become apparent that the process of discovering and litigating fault, whether or not the ultimate issue of truth was ever reached, had become financially burdensome to both sides.

In the wake of the Westmoreland and Sharon cases, both of which were essentially victories for the news media, however, the cost of defending big-league libel suits in the post-Sullivan era became a matter of serious concern for those committed to freedom of the press. In another case involving *Time* Magazine, for example, *Time* agreed to settle a suit with the Schiavone Construction Company, even though the magazine had a good chance of winning. The potential cost of fighting the case all the way through the courts was just too high.

In the euphoria that followed the Sullivan decision, neither side paid much attention to Justice Black's warning in another case: that introducing the concept of fault into libel law would expose the media to potentially ruinous litigation even as it shifted the burden of proof from their shoulders.[5] It must be remembered, however, that for every case in which First Amendment principle falls victim to the financial considerations of media defendants, undoubtedly there are many other instances where the same financial considerations dissuade potential plaintiffs from ever bringing suit.

For all its apparent shortcomings, the present system does at least maintain a balance among the competing interests that is far more delicately calibrated than anything that is likely to emerge from a legislature. The development of libel law since *Sullivan* suggests that truth and fault are equally difficult to prove. If the absolute truth of a statement were any easier to establish than the purity of a journalist's motive or the rigor of his editorial oversight, few libel suits would ever get to trial. But truth, like beauty, is in the eye of the beholder, and determining fault requires highly subjective judgments.

Is it realistic to assume that anyone could ever prove beyond a reasonable doubt whether General Westmoreland conspired to deceive his superiors about the strength of the North Vietnamese army? Can anyone ever establish for certain whether CBS News was out to get him? Can anyone know for sure whether Ariel Sharon encouraged the massacre of Palestinian refugees, or whether the *Time* Magazine correspondent who made that allegation had an ulterior political motive that colored his journalistic objectivity? Conflicts between the press, the public, and the government have been with us for a long time. The tension is natural and healthy for the system. Any proposal to change the way these disputes are resolved must demonstrate first that the current system isn't working, and then show that the alternative would somehow make it work better for all parties.

The best known model for a fresh approach to libel law is the one proposed by a blue-ribbon study committee assembled by The Annenberg Washington Program.[6] The Annenberg proposal is a thoughtful and carefully crafted blueprint for an alternative to the laborious judicial determination of fault that has been a part of libel litigation since the Sullivan decision. But the Annenberg proposal, for all its strengths, leans heavily on the notion that libel plaintiffs are seeking, above all, a timely determination of the truth.

In fact, common sense suggests that most plaintiffs are looking for a vindication of their point of view or, at least, a well-publicized airing of their side of the dispute. Were this not the case, few plaintiffs would have much incentive to challenge the formidable legal barriers that current libel law puts in their path. Furthermore, merely establishing the truth, assuming this is possible in the first place, cannot always restore a plaintiff's good name. Even if it could, the First Amendment guarantees that journalistic freedom and the public's right to know take precedence over the preservation of an individual's reputation. Certainly the evidence suggests that the enormous punitive damage awards that get so much public attention are extremely rare and are usually overturned or significantly reduced on appeal.

The Annenberg plan would allow a libel dispute to be settled immediately with a simple reply or retraction. It does not, however, set down any requirements for length, placement, timing, or any of the other specifications likely to be important to plaintiffs demanding what they believe to be fair treatment. Replies and retractions, of course, already are a part of the dispute resolution process. Nobody knows how many people who feel wronged by a news report, but are not interested in suing for money damages, accept an immediate retraction to settle a dispute with a news outlet. It is doubtful whether the more formal retraction procedure that forms the first step of the Annenberg plan would significantly increase the number of cases settled at this early stage.

Assuming that a reply or retraction is unacceptable to one or both sides, the Annenberg plan offers the news media defendant a tempting bargain with the devil. In exchange for absolute immunity from money damages, a news organization accused of libel can submit itself to a summary judgment of the truth. Accepting a declaratory judgment on the issue of truth relieves the journalist of the risk of enormous punitive damages that a finding of fault might entail. Taking the threat of punitive damages out of the libel equation *does* seem attractive at first glance. But news organizations are usually owned by business people, not journalists. Thus, it might be all too tempting for a manager with an eye on the bottom line to sacrifice constitutional principle, and the long-term credibility of his news franchise, on the altar of short-term financial expediency.

Like the Annenberg proposal, a draft libel law being considered by the Uniform Law Commissioners would separate the determination of truth from the award of damages.[7] Like Annenberg, the proposed uniform libel law assumes that the truth can be clearly determined and that most plaintiffs are concerned above all with seeing the record corrected. Like Annenberg, the proposed uniform law is an attempt to set aside the fault concept and go back to the days before the Sullivan decision when innocent error was punishable as libel.

Unlike Annenberg, however, the proposed uniform law bends over backward to redress what its drafters feel is the current law's unfair bias toward the news media. Its harshest critics view the uniform libel law proposal as nothing more than a clumsy attempt to overturn a quarter century of judicial precedent by tipping the scales of justice back toward the plaintiff's reputational interest, and against the news media's hard-won First Amendment rights.

In addition to the constitutional problems they pose, both the Annenberg plan and the uniform libel law proposal completely ignore the practical problems inherent in any legislative approach to libel law reform. Attempting to pass uniform libel laws in all 50 states is unrealistic. Placing the fate of the free press in the hands of 50 state legislatures is fraught with risk. Legislators at all levels are understandably suspicious of the press. The First Amendment was conceived as a means of making sure not only that ordinary citizens would have the right to speak out against their government, but also that the press would be free to hold government officials and institutions accountable. To circumscribe the free-press protections of the First Amendment by legislative action would do violence to the delicate system of checks and balances upon which the American system depends. In the end, this approach would create more problems than it solves.

Another alternative to current libel law that has received considerable attention is arbitration. While orderly systems of arbitration have been used successfully for many years in other areas, only recently has a serious attempt been made to apply it to libel cases.

The Iowa Libel Research Project studied a long line of libel cases and came to the conclusion that most libel plaintiffs are seeking vindication rather than punitive damages. Out of this research grew the Iowa Libel Dispute Resolution Program[8] set up in cooperation with the American Arbitration Association. Participation in the program is entirely voluntary, and, within broad guidelines, even the procedures themselves are open to negotiation between the parties in each case.

It is easy to see why the Iowa program has been largely ignored. Any dispute that could be resolved by a procedure this flexible probably could have been quickly settled by the parties themselves without outside assistance. If the dispute were sufficiently intractable that the final step of binding arbitration would eventually have to be reached, it is doubtful that the parties would have agreed to an alternative means of resolution in the first place. It is hard to imagine that the parties to a dispute serious enough to require a formal resolution program would be able to negotiate the terms of the proceeding, the crucial first step in the Iowa process. The notion that the parties in a serious dispute over defamation of character will agree to waive legal recourse and sit down with one another to work out an amicable arbitration arrangement is, at best, Utopian.

Long before either arbitration schemes or statutory reform proposals were put forward as substitutes for current libel law, the National News Council was set up as an alternative to traditional means of resolving disputes over news coverage. The council was born in an era of great controversy over the proper role of the news media in American society. From its inception, the council was promoted as the media's last best hope of recovering their damaged credibility and fending off political assaults on their patriotism. Unfortunately for the council, the media organizations it proposed to protect largely ignored it. Some were downright hostile. As a result, the council spent its short, unhappy life trying without success to win the respect and support of the very institution it was supposed to be monitoring and criticizing. It died in obscurity without ever having addressed any but the most trivial journalistic issues.

The National News Council is gone, but a similar organization survives in Minnesota. The Minnesota News Council has received generally high marks for its work, but it, too, lives hand to mouth, struggling against a tide of public indifference and media hostility.

As an alternative to libel litigation, news councils enjoy one important advantage. They can, and do, deal with issues of news media behavior that fall outside the scope of libel law. The Minnesota News Council, for example, has dealt with cases in which news organizations have gone back on informal agreements not to print the names of witnesses to violent crimes. There are no legal questions involved in cases like these, but hearings held by the council not only satisfy members of the public who feel the press has invaded their privacy, but can also cause news organizations to review and improve their procedures. Even its critics concede that the Minnesota News Council has done some good work, especially in cases like these where fairness and good manners, rather than defamation of character or actionable invasion of privacy, are at issue.

News councils, of course, lack any enforcement power. They are entirely voluntary and can easily degenerate into little more than debating societies. To have any effect at all, news councils must earn the respect of both the news media and the public, and the outcome of their proceedings must receive widespread publicity. Unfortunately, this rarely happens. The National News Council operated during a period of unprecedented public debate about the role of the news media in our society, but few outside the journalistic community even knew the council existed. The Minnesota News Council has labored in similar obscurity for almost 20 years.

At their best, news councils offer the general public a quick and effective safety valve, a forum for their complaints about the press, and a way to get attention for their point of view. But without enforcement power on the one hand, or the opportunity to generate widespread publicity on the other, no news council, national or local, is likely to satisfy a plaintiff's thirst for vindication. Only a well-publicized, big-money libel suit, even if it is eventually unsuccessful, can do that.

If news councils in the United States have been obscure, across the Atlantic the British Press Council is anything but. It has long been a respected forum for the resolution of media disputes, and it is now at the center of a contentious and highly political public debate over press responsibility. While the British constitution has never accorded the news media the privileges granted by our First Amendment, the evolution of the British Press Council is, nonetheless, an interesting example of both the good that news councils can do, and the dangers they can pose.

After years of public complaints about the excesses of the tabloid press, and not a few bitter confrontations between the more serious news organizations and the government, a parliamentary commission recently released a report calling on the British press voluntarily to invest a press council with strong enforcement powers. If the media refuse, or if the newly empowered press council proves ineffective, the report recommends that Parliament create a government-appointed tribunal to hear and settle disputes between the media and the public with the full force of law.

This, of course, is the dark side of the news council concept. Not only could a body of news council precedents be used to throttle the media in court, but, without the First Amendment to protect them, the media could easily find themselves subjected to judgments far more severe than those under current law.

Looking, then, at the three principal types of reform proposals that have been developed over the years, none seems capable of improving on the system already in place, imperfect as it is. Statutory reforms like the Annenberg plan and the Uniform Law Commission proposal are not only impractical but pose an entirely unwarranted risk to hard-won First Amendment rights. On close examination, they neither address the legitimate concerns of the public nor calm the fears of the press.

Arbitration presumably would work as well in libel cases as it has in other types of disputes, but the dismal experience of the Iowa program suggests that parties on both sides of consequential disputes are inclined to take their chances in the courts. They are not likely to waive legal recourse on the chance that they can receive a fair hearing in a loosely organized arbitration proceeding.

Notwithstanding the Iowa Project's research findings, the practical evidence suggests that a significant number of plaintiffs are more than willing to navigate the treacherous waters of the legal system in order to gain publicity for their point of view and to punish the media with expensive litigation, even in a losing cause.

News councils, as long as they lack enforcement powers or at least universal acceptance and media support, are doomed to operate in the shadows. It took the British Press Council more than a quarter of a century to gain prominence and earn respect. Even now, if the council is given any real power it will only be under the threat of legislative action that in this country would be flatly unconstitutional.

To those who fear the power of the news media, the truth is not of utmost importance. For them, judgment, interpretation, journalistic practice, and what they perceive to be fairness are the real issues. No new libel law, no reconstituted National News Council, no arbitration scheme can possibly satisfy the political agendas of these special interests without eviscerating the First Amendment.

The U.S. Constitution quite properly makes the news media responsible only to themselves and their customers. The American media are not responsible to the government. Journalists will always remain outsiders, accountable only to their readers, listeners, and viewers. A journalist's best defense against a charge of unfairness has always been to do his job and let the public judge the product. The First Amendment lets the American people judge both the fairness of the press and the credibility of its antagonists. Free of unconstitutional restraint, the news media will do their job, and the marketplace will continue to punish journalists who go too far. In any event, big-ticket libel suits seem to be on the decline. While this may suggest that the news media are backing off, it may also be the natural result of potential plaintiffs thinking twice before spending millions on a lost cause. A balance has been struck.

If our libel laws are broken, we should fix them, but before we travel down the road to reform we should make very sure that the trip is necessary. Before we fundamentally change our way of dealing with disputes about news coverage, we should make sure that we are making the most of the rules we already have in place. Until it can be shown that reform would significantly improve on the system we already have, imperfect as it is, we should leave well enough alone. The First Amendment is far too valuable to risk in an effort to solve a problem that probably doesn't exist.

Notes

[1] Johnston, Harry M., III and Kaufman, Henry R., "Annenberg, *Sullivan* at twenty-five, and the question of libel reform," *Communications Lawyer: A Publication of the Forum on Communications Law*, American Bar Association, Vol. 7, No. 1, Winter 1989, p. 8.

[2] *Gitlow v. New York*, 268 U.S. 652 (1925).

[3] *Cox v. Louisiana*, 379 U.S. 559 (1965).

[4] *New York Times Co. v. Sullivan*, 376 U.S. 254 (1964).

[5] *Curtis Publishing Co. v. Butts*, 388 U.S. 130 (1967).

[6] *Proposal for the Reform of Libel Law: The Report of the Libel Reform Project of The Annenberg Washington Program*, (Washington: The Annenberg Washington Program in Communications Policy Studies of Northwestern University, 1988). *See also* the essay by Richard M. Schmidt, Jr., in this book at Chapter 3, pp. 65-82.

[7] Drafting Committee on Defamation Act, *Draft Defamation Act*, (Chicago: Uniform Law Commissioners, July 1990).

[8] Cranberg, Gilbert, "Libel judges are setting standards for the press," *Washington Journalism Review*, Vol. 11, No. 7, Sept. 1989, p. 42. *See also* the essay by John Soloski and Roselle L. Wissler in this book at Chapter 4, pp. 83-111.

VI. The British Press Council Experience

Kenneth Morgan

On the afternoon of Tuesday, July 21, 1953, in London, England, the General Council of the Press met for the first time. It was a voluntary body, formed and paid for by the press itself, not imposed by or answerable to government; it was Britain's answer to the problem of preserving the freedom of the press while at the same time trying to ensure its responsibility, and to resolve the grievances of those who felt they had been wronged.

Thirty-seven years later on the afternoon of Tuesday, June 28, 1990, the Press Council met in London to discuss the report of a government-appointed committee which recommended its abolition. The report,[1] accepted instantly by the Conservative government and the Labor opposition, called for the Press Council to be replaced by a Press Complaints Commission.

This, too, the report said, should be set up and paid for by the press itself. It should deal only with complaints against newspapers; but, significantly, it would have no role in defending their freedom. Reporting to Parliament and to the Home Secretary, the Committee on Privacy and Related Matters, chaired by Mr. David Calcutt QC (a leading lawyer and head of a Cambridge college), described its recommendation as newspapers' final chance to prove that self-regulation could be made to work.

So far, perhaps, so good. But if in someone's opinion (the report did not say whose) the last chance failed, the non-statutory complaints commission would be replaced by a statutory commission with new powers of law over the press. In the worst case it would be replaced by a statutory complaints tribunal—a judge appointed by the Lord Chancellor sitting with two assessors appointed by the Home Secretary, ruling whether newspapers were in breach of a statutory code of practice to be "drafted by the Government in consultation with the press and other interested parties."

The story of how a freedom-cherishing democratic society moved from its position in 1953 to its position in 1990 is the story of the British Press Council. Press councils are not in fact a British invention. Long before 1953 recognizable ancestors had been founded, in Norway in 1912 and in Sweden in 1916. If the British Press Council is the father of press councils in Australia, New Zealand, Canada, and many less likely places, those councils have Scandinavian grandparents in Norway and Sweden, to say nothing of great aunts in Denmark and Finland.

In its international spread, however, the press council movement owes a great deal to British example. To understand it, and its successes and failures as a device for settling conflict between the media and those who feel they have been wronged, the differences between legal and cultural attitudes toward the press in Britain and America need to be kept in mind.

Unlike the United States, Britain has no First Amendment. More importantly in some ways, she has nothing to which she could make a First Amendment were she so minded. No written constitution, no bill of rights; even the European Declaration of Human Rights forms no part of her law. Unlike most of Europe, she is, and certainly was in 1953, a common-law country building up much of her law by decisions of her judges as she went along rather than laying it down in advance in the form of a code. Over recent decades that has begun to change.

Her press had then and has still no guarantee of freedom, although in practice it remains freer than newspapers in much of the rest of the world. Britain has made do without any significant body of special press law: Newspapers are unlicensed, journalists are unregistered, and neither have much in the way of special privileges or special responsibilities beyond those of the ordinary enterprise and the ordinary citizen. That is no matter for complaint but a situation to welcome, but I fear that it, too, has begun to change. Such change is of particular concern in a country without the constitutional protection of a First Amendment—a country which, again significantly, has an Official Secrets Act but no Freedom of Information Act.

Against the background of unprotected but generally accepted freedom of the press, Britain chose in 1949 to set up a voluntary press council rather than a piece of state machinery to try to resolve the conflict of a society which wants a free press but expects it to be responsible.

Britain and her politicians were concerned at the state of her press at the end of World War II. They were concerned then at the growing tendency toward concentration of ownership which was less marked than it is now, and at the ethical standards of newspaper proprietors and journalists. Well before that, though, there had been what I see as a healthy adversarial relationship between politicians and the press. In the 1930s Stanley Baldwin made the most celebrated criticism of the papers by a politician:

> Their methods are direct falsehood, misrepresentation, half-truths, the alteration of a speaker's meaning by putting sentences apart from the context, suppression and editorial criticism of speeches which are not reported in the paper. What the proprietorship of these papers is aiming at is power, but power without responsibility—the prerogative of the harlot through the ages.[2]

It was not a criticism fueled by party conflict, but a statement by a Conservative leader about two Conservative press barons, Lord Beaverbrook and Lord Rothermere. Appropriately enough when speaking of a press often criticized for publishing ghost-written material, the words were not Baldwin's own but supplied by his cousin, Rudyard Kipling—a journalist. They remain, however, a fair catalogue of the principal charges leveled even now against the British popular press—if one adds intrusion into privacy.

Baldwin's criticism was echoed after World War II in the much more general concern about newspaper conduct which led Parliament to set up the first Royal Commission on the Press. The Commission recommended to the newspaper industry that it establish a General Council of the Press to defend the press's freedom and maintain its professional standards.[3] The name carried a deliberate echo of the General Medical Council which exercised professional control over medicine, but an important difference was suggested. The GMC was based in statute; the General Council of the Press (later renamed the Press Council) was to derive its authority not from the law but from the press itself. The Royal Commission believed the council should be a voluntary body relying on influence rather than power.

At that time Britain stood firmer than she appears to now in her liberal and libertarian tradition that the contents of newspapers, while a proper subject for public concern, were an inappropriate one for state action or determination by positive law. While holding to that view, the Royal Commission's recommendation was an early affirmation that the contents of privately owned newspapers and the conduct of journalists were the legitimate concern of those they wrote for and about, as well as of those who owned and edited them.

It was Britain's rejection of W.P. Hamilton's classic American definition of a private enterprise press:

> A newspaper is a private enterprise owing nothing whatever to the public, which grants it no franchise. It is therefore affected with no public interest. It is emphatically the property of the owner, who is selling a manufactured product at his own risk.[4]

From that rejection and the birth of the Press Council there developed the consensus, recognized over 30 years later by the third Royal Commission on the Press, that the press should neither be subjected to state control nor left to the unregulated forces of the market. The

Press Council's role has been to hold that balance, and with it also the balance between the free press people cherish and the responsible press they demand. "I am with you on the freedom of the press," they repeat, with the character out of Tom Stoppard's play "Night and Day." "It's the newspapers I can't stand."

This consensus and the need to strike the balance produced the British Press Council. Its birth was not easy. Reporting in 1949, the first Royal Commission recommended a council consisting of members from the newspaper owners', editors', and journalists' organizations, with lay members representing the general public—newspaper readers—and an independent chairman. But there was no instant enthusiasm in the newspaper industry to set up a council at all, and the only organization initially in favor of including lay members was the National Union of Journalists. After more than two years of talk, it took a nudge from government and an implied threat to impose a statutory council to get agreement on the size, shape, and scope of a voluntary one. When it came it was not the council dreamed of by the first Royal Commission. No public members, no voice of the readers, but 25 publishers, editors, and journalists. It had no independent chairman from outside the press as the Commission had suggested, but a chairman elected from around the board. He, almost predictably in English terms at that time, was the principal proprietor of the *Times*, Col. the Hon. J.J. Astor.

In the 37 years since its foundation in that form in 1953 the council's scope, its profile, and its workload have changed markedly but its objects, set out in its constitution, have been constant:
- to preserve the established freedom of the British press; to maintain its character in accordance with the highest professional and commercial standards;
- to consider complaints about its conduct or the conduct of others toward it, and deal with these in a practical and appropriate manner; and
- to keep under review developments likely to restrict the supply of information of public interest and importance; and to report publicly on developments toward greater concentration or monopoly in the press.[5]

In general and sometimes in detail these objects have been adopted in other countries where press councils have been founded on the British model. The first two objects lead to the Press Council being compared to a watchdog with two heads barking in opposite directions: one to give warning to the press when its freedom is in danger; the other barking at the press when its freedom is abused. The image of the watchdog is valuable, but now for the first time is at risk with both the British government and the official opposition accepting in principle the Calcutt Committee's recommendation that one of the dog's heads be struck off, leaving determination of complaints against newspapers to a body which has no similar duty to defend their freedom.

Before the last 12 months there had been two fundamental revisions of the council since its foundation. The first was after 10 years in 1963 when, on the advice of a second Royal Commission, public members were introduced, at first very tentatively in the proportion of five public to 20 press. At the same time, much more wholeheartedly, the council accepted the Royal Commission's recommendation to appoint an independent chairman unconnected with the press. It has now had six, all of them lawyers, starting with Lord Devlin, a distinguished and admired member of the highest tier of the British judiciary, a Lord of Appeal.

Lord Devlin summarized what he described as the six pillars or factors of a successful voluntary press council anywhere:
(1) The press itself must generally accept that a press council is a desirable thing to have.
(2) The government of the country, whatever its form, must be responsive to public opinion and must accept that the press has a constitutional part to play in forming and expressing opinion.
(3) The press must accept a corresponding obligation: There must be standards of conduct to which the press conforms, though Lord Devlin emphasized that this did not necessarily mean a written code or rules enforceable by pains and penalties—a proviso which has been much discussed and argued over since.
(4) Each newspaper must accept the obligation to publish adjudications by the press council against itself.

(5) The public must be represented on the press council.
(6) The council's function is to stand up for the freedom and rights of the press as well as to censure its misconduct.[6]

He saw things more clearly and surely than some of his successors in other public offices. Each of his six points identified a crucial issue in the structure of self-regulation of the press and its partnership with the public which has deeply concerned journalists and jurists, publishers and public.

The second major review of the council came in 1978 after an inquiry by a third Royal Commission on the Press, chaired by Lord McGregor of Durris, university professor of social institutions, and later chairman of Britain's Advertising Standards Authority and of the Reuter Trustees.

His report matched Lord Devlin's six pillars of a press council with three signposts for councils:

- The press council plays a key role in maintaining public confidence in the press, and a basic condition for such confidence is that it must be wholly independent of government.
- The press council must also show a determination to be independent of the press. The public will not believe that a council dominated by journalists and others from the press can keep an effective watch on the standards of the press or can deal satisfactorily with complaints by citizens.
- Finally, an effective press council must be expert and influential enough for its judgment to carry weight within the press, with proprietors, editors, and journalists.[7]

Thirteen years later the signposts still point in the right direction. In fact it took 25 years from the council's inception to get the proportion of press and public membership right. In 1978, following the McGregor Commission's advice, the balance was evened—18 press members and 18 public members, with an independent, voting chairman to tip it slightly to the public or non-press side. In fact, the early political concern among journalists and publishers about first the existence, and then the growth, of a lay element on the council has proved misplaced. It has never divided on any issue along party lines with the public members voting one way and the press members the other. As in examples of self-regulation in other professions, practitioners, rather than the laity, have frequently proved harder critics of incompetence or unethical behavior by their colleagues and competitors.

Throughout the council's life its press members have been appointed in agreed proportions by their own organizations of publishers, editors, and journalists. It is more difficult to devise machinery to select 18 members of the public to represent 56 million. Originally the choice was made by the council itself. Recently, a separate appointments commission has chosen from among candidates who volunteer or are nominated by anyone or any organization in response to an annual invitation by the council. The only qualification: Those considered must have no editorial or managerial connection with the press. The aim is that members be drawn from as varied social, occupational, and geographical backgrounds as possible, and broadly that aim has been achieved.

From being criticized 20 years ago as too often middle-aged, middle-class, male, and white, they have come over recent years to represent different ages, sexes, and ethnic groups. They have included a former assistant commissioner of the City of London Police, a trading standards officer, a woman professor now a member of the House of Lords, a mountaineering school leader, a boilermaker, a former clerk of the Queen's Privy Council, Roman Catholic, Anglican, and Methodist ministers, a nurse, and a distinguished surgeon; Scots, Welsh, Irish, an Asian, and an Afro-Caribbean, as well as English; usually 10 or 11 men and seven or eight women.

One measure of the success or acceptability of a voluntary institution is the willingness of people to serve it. Press and public members of the Press Council work hard, having to allocate to it and its committees two or three days each month and much reading time. They get no fees although their expenses are paid. The involvement of editors, journalists, and owners on those terms may be something one can expect; the sacrifice of members of the public on such terms is remarkable. When the present, open nomination procedure was introduced in 1978 there were 44 candidates for 10 public seats. On the last selection the appointments commission had to choose six members from a field of 1,036.

So far, it has been significant and important that in Britain neither the government nor Parliament has played any part in the nomination or selection of members of the council. It is not so everywhere. There are different traditions, and press councils tend to inherit the characteristics of their countries, in the way that the British Press Council inherited the English tradition of common law rather than codified law. India inherited (confusingly, and embarrassingly enough from its British imperial masters) a substantial code of special press law. In that spirit, its press council (though otherwise very similar to Britain's) is established by law, not as a voluntary body. As a result, a proportion of its public members are appointed by Parliament to represent the political parties.

Similarly, since the restoration of democracy in 1974 until this year, Portugal had a *Conselho de Imprensa* which was in its own phrase "inspired by Great Britain's Press Council." The law provided, however, that its members should include "four citizens with acknowledged merits elected by the Assembly of the Republic." In Britain so far, the only time a government minister ever nominated a candidate for the Press Council, the minister (acting in his private capacity) was the Home Secretary and his nominee was not appointed.

Change is now on the march. In Portugal this year a new constitutional law has abolished the old statutory Press Council in favor of a wider statutory media authority. Responding to the British Press Council's protest at this in supporting its old Portuguese ally, the Portuguese government said there were moves afoot there by publishers and newspaper unions to found a truly voluntary press council which would be independent of the state—more similar, they said, to the Press Council in Great Britain.

Meanwhile, however, the British government was accepting the Calcutt report which proposes a Press Complaints Commission whose members would be chosen by an appointments commission selected "perhaps by the Lord Chancellor"—the only member of the British judiciary who is also a member of the Cabinet and a party political appointee.

Members of the current British Press Council, whether appointed by the press organizations or selected to represent the public, sit together with equal rights and duties on the council itself and on one of its three complaints committees. (There is a fourth committee, the General Purposes Committee, which deals with the press-freedom side of the business, likely now to be lost under the Calcutt proposals.) In recent years Britain has been fortunate in the way in which press and public members have meshed together; it has not been so in the press councils of all countries.

Recently chance brought the executive secretary of the Australian Press Council and the secretary of the Press Council of British Columbia to London at the same time. Both attended a British complaints committee meeting, where members were cross-examining witnesses called by the complainant and the editor and then considering their verdict. Afterward, the Australian and the Canadian both said the most striking difference was that they could not tell whether a speaker was a press member or a public member by the questions he put or the comments he made. An encouraging judgment.

So far the role of the complaints committees has been to consider written (and sometimes oral) evidence and arguments about each complaint, and then to recommend an adjudication to the full Press Council which accepts, rejects, or amends it. As part of a major review of the council's own function conducted over the last year, however, it is now proposed that complaints committees should be empowered in the future to reach their own adjudications on cases without further reference to the full council, except where the case is of special significance or where the committee's finding is challenged and appealed to the council.

In Britain, any person or organization may complain to the Press Council about the contents or conduct of any newspaper or magazine which is available to the general public. In some countries, including Sweden, the right to complain is limited to those directly affected by the newspaper item contested: A complainant must have standing. The same restrictive rule applies in Britain to the statutory Broadcasting Complaints Commission. In the interests of encouraging high general standards of press conduct, I am in favor of an unrestricted right for the public at large to complain at their infraction, but the open complaints system practiced in Britain does produce problems. Most obviously, it can lead to difficulties where a complaint is made by a third party about press intrusion into someone else's privacy. The Press Council finds itself having to tread a difficult path to avoid becoming a second intruder into that same privacy.

Whether third-party complaints of this kind should be entertained perhaps hinges on whether a press council's principal aim is the general one of encouraging and maintaining high professional and ethical standards in the press, or the more specific one of providing a means of redress for those whom the press has wronged. Each is valuable to society and it is possible to do both—but harder than doing only one, and the risk increases that the council's role will be misunderstood.

In practice, the great majority of the British Press Council's complaints (1,484 received and 1,871 handled last year) are complaints by individuals or organizations who believe they have been directly wronged by the conduct of a journalist or an item in a newspaper or magazine—or sometimes the refusal to publish an item (*e.g.*, a letter). The smaller proportion of more general "for-the-public-good" complaints included in those totals (and about half the complaints which run full distance and are adjudicated) are likely to raise a political point, an issue of taste, treatment of race, or perhaps use of language. An open complaints system does not restrict the right to complain to British citizens; in fact, the all-comers record for making the greatest number of complaints to the British Press Council is held by a Chicagoan, resident in London, Bob Borzello. Six years ago he took on the mantle of conscience or prosecutor of the British press in respect of its treatment of race and later of sex and sexual orientation.

Since then he has made over 220 complaints to the Press Council, almost none of them directly involving reference to himself. He is criticized by some editors as a "vexatious complainant." The description can hardly be apt: In the courts vexatious litigants do not win—before the Press Council Borzello does, too often for editors' comfort. Indeed on the race issue, he has been largely responsible for mending British newspapers' manners in a surprisingly short time.

Press councils judge complaints on the basis of ethics, not law. Inevitably, however, there is some overlap. Libel is the obvious example. A defamatory newspaper article is almost certainly unethical. By one route, the civil courts, a person defamed may seek and receive heavy damages—perhaps over £1 million—but to do so he must risk heavy costs. By complaining to the Press Council he can hope only to put the record straight, clear his name, and see the newspaper publicly rebuked and possibly censured. But he may do this at virtually no cost, and no risk of costs.

The ability of people to do that is especially important where libel is not only a particularly expensive (or for the lawyer, lucrative) branch of the law, but is, as in Britain, almost the only branch of civil law where there is no state aid for the poor man who brings or defends an action.

The danger is that an aggrieved reader who has the means to sue may seek both remedies, using the cheap route of one to enhance his chances of obtaining the financial rewards of the other. To avoid this when a complaint is made and it looks likely that a libel action may also be mounted, the Press Council asks the complainant to sign a waiver of legal action. It is a controversial course. Over the years, generations of editors and lawyers, two royal commissions, and parliamentary committees have argued the wisdom and justification for seeking waivers. The arguments are finely balanced. On one side: What right has a voluntary organization to stand between a free-born Englishman (or a guy from Chicago, come to that) and his right to sue in the Queen's courts? On the other, what editor in his right mind is going to disclose in an inquiry into a Press Council complaint information which may then be used against him in a libel action? The Press Council has reviewed the question many times but has found that so far the practical need for a waiver prevails. Now to the dismay of editors the Calcutt Committee has recommended that its proposed press complaints commission should operate without asking complainants to waive their right to sue.

There are ways through or round the problem but they may not be to everyone's taste. The Press Council encounters some complainants who demur at waiving their rights. In such cases the council defers consideration, advising the complainant to go and do his suing first, returning for the Press Council to consider any ethical issues left outstanding after the legal carcass of the case has been picked clean in the courts.

The other obvious alternative is to follow the example of the British Broadcasting Complaints Commission. It is barred from dealing with a complaint for which a legal remedy is available in the courts. That is one way over the problem but hardly an acceptable one so long as the libel law remains only a rich man's remedy. The poor have their reputations too.

Defamation is only one area of complaint with which the Press Council deals. The most common is inaccuracy, and others include the right to publish, right of reply, objections to comment (a generally unfruitful area, for newspapers are entitled to be partisan), matters of taste (including the use of pictures and sometimes cartoons), selection of news (another unfruitful area, for editors must be expected to edit), methods of newsgathering (including the use, or abuse, of subterfuge), unacceptable checkbook journalism, unjustifiable intrusion into privacy, the treatment of letters to the editor, and some issues about advertisements and the conduct of newspaper competitions.

Two of those areas of press criticism have assumed a particular importance in recent years to the extent of putting the future of self-regulation of the press in doubt. Britain has no law similar to those common among European countries requiring newspapers to correct inaccuracies or to give aggrieved parties a right of reply. Similarly but somewhat surprisingly Britain has no law protecting individual privacy as many other countries do. The Press Council has long maintained that there is an ethical obligation on newspapers to afford the one when asked and respect the other, but no law says they must do so. Several attempts to establish a right-of-reply and a protection-of-privacy law have been made by private members in the House of Commons over the last six or seven years.

It was the progress made by two such bills last year, right-of-reply by a Labor member and protection-of-privacy by a Tory, which led the British government to set up the Committee on Privacy and Related Matters under Mr. David Calcutt QC to consider whether there should be new laws, and whether changes were needed in the redress available to citizens aggrieved by newspapers. Announcing the Committee's appointment in April 1989, the Home Office Minister of State, Mr. Tim Renton MP, told the House: "The press is on probation." In the following nine months the Press Council pursued a vigorous review of its own role and function, discussing self-regulation with all the organizations of publishers, editors, and journalists; the council departed from its common-law approach to frame a formal code of practice for the first time. In addition, 19 national newspaper editors from the *Times*, the *Independent*, and the *Guardian* to the *Sun* and the *Daily Star* met to agree to a mini five-point code and announce that they would each (with one exception, the *Financial Times*) appoint reader's representatives or ombudsmen to deal with complaints which could also then be pursued to the Press Council.

When it has tried a complaint either at first instance or following an ombudsman's initial bite, what can a press council do? In Britain and most other countries where they exist: announce its finding—uphold or reject the complaint and state its reasons for the decision, perhaps censuring the paper or its editor.

In Britain the adjudication is released generally for publication in all except a small minority of cases usually involving personal privacy or perhaps the identification of a child. The council gets good general publicity for its adjudications in the regional press and reasonable coverage in the serious national press. Importantly for the council, its adjudications are published regularly and fairly fully in the main professional weekly for journalists. The great majority are carried very fully on the wire service of the Press Association which goes into virtually every British daily newspaper office.

Most importantly, there is a particular obligation on the editor of any newspaper or magazine which is the subject of a critical adjudication to publish that adjudication word for word in its own columns. It is a moral obligation, not a legal one, but it is almost universally observed. There have been only 11 occasions in 33 years when a newspaper or magazine found to be at fault has failed to honor the obligation, and in almost all those cases the publication concerned was a fringe journal rather than one of the general body of the British commercial national or regional press.

Where concern lies is more often at the way in which a critical adjudication is published than whether it is published. Every newspaperman knows where one hides an item which has to be published but preferably not read. In its recent review the Press Council decided that judgments should more often include instructions—again with moral but not legal force—about the prominence the judgments should be given in the paper.

If a paper fails to publish a critical adjudication, the Press Council issues a second adjudication condemning it again for its original fault but condemning it more harshly for not honoring an obligation which the press in general accepts. As a rule, journals other than the defaulter prove happy to publish adjudications of this kind about their competitor and to publish them prominently!

There is a difference here between the British, Australian, Canadian, and New Zealand approach and those of some other countries. Under its statutory powers, for example, the Indian press council may obtain an order from the courts requiring a newspaper to publish an adverse adjudication. In fact the power of the court order is illusory, for it is without means of enforcement. On the face of it, however, such a second-stage link between self-regulation by a press council and ultimate reliance on the power of the courts might appear attractive—but not, one hopes, to an American mind. One prime danger in the possible link between self-regulation and statutory British press regulation (however limited) as proposed by the Calcutt Committee is that generations do not bind their successors. The narrow purpose for an Indian bridge between the realms of moral obligation and legal enforcement might just be tolerable, but none of us can know which men and which measures might come crowding across that bridge behind us.

It is a chilling thought—more chilling than Mr. Renton's "the press is on probation"—that Britain has reached the point of considering measures well beyond the "Indian" enforcement-of-publication proposition with talk of a statutory complaints commission and even of a statutory tribunal enforcing a statutory code. Assuming a voluntary press council in any country—under whatever name—critics of the press will continue to argue for it to have stronger sanctions, sharper teeth than the embarrassment of publicity on which Britain's and the others have relied so far. One is entitled to ask the press critics what they have in mind. It is not easy to see how a voluntary body standing apart from a country's legal system could be given the sort of penal powers that appear to be envisaged except under contractual arrangements between the press council and the publishers.

That apart, there are practical and philosophical problems about the nature of alternative, stronger sanctions. What might those sanctions be? The first and most obvious is the power to fine. It is difficult to envisage a sufficiently varied tariff of fines which could be imposed on offenders as varied as the national daily newspapers selling millions, give-away local weeklies, learned journals, and teenage magazines with which the Press Council in London deals, which would be fair and an effective deterrent to each of them. The severe criticism of British newspapers which fuels calls for stronger sanctions against misconduct is not criticism of local or regional newspapers for inaccuracy or lapses of taste.

It is criticism of a very small number of very high-selling national daily and Sunday papers at the rough end of the tabloid trade, and it is criticism of them for alleged fabrication or unwarranted intrusion into privacy. If an economic penalty were to be relied upon, as deterrent, the fines would need to be of hundreds of thousands of pounds. Anything less, and the likelihood is that the intended deterrent would become merely a (tax deductible?) operating expense. One of the oldest press councils, Sweden's, does impose fines on erring newspapers but, practically, not so much as a deterrent but as an acceptable revenue raiser for the press council itself.

The next grade up from fines in deterrent sanctions which even some relatively civilized politicians in Britain will now suggest, is the licensing and registration sanction. What, they ask, could be wrong with a press council suspending a newspaper for publication for a few days, perhaps a week or two, for irresponsibility? Alternatively, suspending an erring journalist from the register and denying him work or publication as a punishment? The appropriate response is to say "If you do not know what is wrong with that, go to, say, Chile, Czechoslovakia, or South Africa and ask someone with a memory. He or she will know what is wrong with a nation licensing its press, registering its journalists, and relying on the threat of rescinding the license or striking the name from the register to enforce compliance."

The only obvious third and most severe sanction, then, is to follow a common-enough international example: Send the occasional editor to prison for the same reason that the British once (according to Voltaire) shot one of their own admirals, *pour encourager les autres*.[8]

In the recurring argument about press conduct and appropriate penalties over the last 30 years, I had thought reliance on that ultimate sanction could be ruled out. But now, alongside a potential statutory press complaints commission or tribunal, the Calcutt Committee recommends the creation for the first time of new criminal offenses of which, effectively, only journalists could be found guilty. The new crimes proposed are entering private property without consent "with intent to obtain personal information with a view to its publication," placing a surveillance device on private property for a similar purpose, or taking a picture or recording the voice of a person on private property with a view to publication.

One does not need to condone invasion of privacy, surreptitious surveillance, or sneak photography to worry at these activities being translated from the sphere of ethics to crime. Those who wrote the report and those who have now adopted it in principle no doubt intend only to threaten criminal sanctions on journalists, not to impose them. The danger is real that ultimately some unfortunate photographer or reporter will fetch up in gaol in England.

No doubt if the state finds that it has, almost inadvertently, put some journalist in prison, the state will bend all its energies and summon all its forensic ingenuity to find a way of getting him out again with the minimum of fuss and, if possible, without the embarrassing paraphernalia of martyrdom. Once such laws are there it can be easier to get people into prison than to get them out. Special laws effectively designating journalists a peculiarly imprisonable class are too dangerous to have lying around—even if proposed and enacted naively with good intent.

Not fines? Not licensing and suspension? Not imprisonment? The conclusion is that the most appropriate and acceptable safeguard against the evils of publicity by a free press is—publicity itself. Therefore the sanction which most press councils now have—publication of a critical adjudication, and particularly self-publication of it by the newspaper at fault—is the right sanction.

Accepting this means, in practice, recognizing that part of the price of preserving a free press while cherishing a responsible press is the toleration of some measure of irresponsibility. It means recognizing too, however, that there is a limit to what measure of irresponsibility a public—or a parliament—will stand.

There are signs, much clearer than before, that Britain is close to that line. The question arises whether self-regulation by a voluntary press council or a voluntary press complaints commission—the name does not really matter—can satisfy the critics and survive in a recognizable form.

The Press Council itself, in its own review, has taken a pruning knife and suggests a sensible cut in its size from 36 plus a chairman to 24. More significantly, it would breach the direct link with newspaper bodies—publishers, editors, and journalists—by having its 12 new press members selected by a commission of experienced newspaper and magazine men and women instead of nominated to council seats directly by the press organizations.

The council would keep its waiver but controversially would introduce a "hot-line." Complainants fearful of invasion of their privacy would be able to phone the council's director who would put an editor on notice of complaint before his reporter or photographer moved in. This has sparked a controversy because this is the nearest that self-regulation has come to prior restraint. "Too much. It goes too far," many editors felt. But their chorus was rebutted by the Calcutt Committee's verdict that while the Press Council's review proposals were a welcome step in the right direction, they did not go far enough.

The Calcutt recipe is for a much smaller Press Complaints Commission: a chairman and 12 members with no precise parity or agreed proportion between press and public members, but the proviso that the press members be drawn from "senior editorial levels" and the lay members be "people of high calibre." The commission, voluntary in concept, would become statutory, or be replaced by a statutory tribunal if the newspaper industry dragged its feet or defaulted.

More disturbingly, the conversion to a statutory commission with power to require publication of findings and corrections and to award compensation against newspapers would be triggered by a "maverick publication" persistently declining to respect the voluntary Press Complaints Commission's authority. The practical effect is to require every newspaper editor to stand surety for the good behavior of every other editor—with the continuation of self-regulation as the bail money.

The initial voluntary commission would abandon the waiver of legal proceedings; it would adopt the Press Council's proposed hot line, converting it into a 24-hour-a-day service. In addition, its progenitor, the Calcutt Committee, offers newspapers and journalists a new code of practice clearly rewritten from the Press Council code. Journalism in Britain has thus been the beneficiary of three new codes in eight months: Calcutt's, the Press Council's, and the national newspaper editors', joining those which the National Union of Journalists and the Institute of Journalists have had all along. The difference with the latest is that it can become a law, enforceable ultimately by the courts, if someone puts a foot wrong.

Britain's Press Council does not stand alone. Its sons, daughters, and successors in other parts of the world from the old commonwealth to Papua-New Guinea and Turkey watch what is going on with interest. In November 1989 in Kuala Lumpur, press councils from throughout the world agreed in principle to the drafting of a constitution for a proposed World Association of Press Councils.

In response to the Calcutt Report and the British government's reaction to it, Professor David Flint, chairman of the Australian Press Council and a member of the pro tem committee developing a World Association constitution, said:

> Great Britain is still seen as a model for many countries. Throughout the centuries, the freedoms that the British people have enjoyed have made her a beacon, a land where,

at times almost totally surrounded by tyranny, freedom of speech and a free press have flourished.

Those British ideas on liberty and her free institutions have been successfully transplanted to many other lands. One such institution is the free press. Another is the Press Council itself.[9]

His view is that the central flaw of the Calcutt Report is its failure to accept the basic proposition that freedom of speech and of the press, and the requirement that the press be responsible, form a single, indivisible concept. They are in fact the two sides of one coin. As Professor Flint put it: "An irresponsible press abuses and debases its freedom, but there is no requirement for responsibility by a press that does not enjoy freedom."[10]

The great danger for Britain's press is that irritation and annoyance with the excesses of a few highly profitable papers have put at risk the future of reliance on voluntary self-regulation for the resolution of its conflicts—by a press council or a press complaints commission (the name is almost immaterial). In a proper determination to protect individual privacy from unjustifiable intrusion, the Calcutt Committee may not only have proposed the risky creation of three new criminal offenses, but may also have encouraged society itself to commit a fourth—demanding ethics with menaces.

The Calcutt Committee's recipe is described as a last chance for self-regulation of the press. Inevitably there is the question of whether its product can still be called self-regulation.

Notes

1. Home Office, *Report of the Committee on Privacy and Related Matters*, (London: Her Majesty's Stationery Office, June 1990), Cm. 1102.

2. Stanley Baldwin, 1st Earl Baldwin of Bewdley; speech at Queen's Hall, London, St. George's Westminster by-election March 17, 1930, quoted in Koss, Stephen, *The Rise and Fall of the Political Press in Britain, Vol. 2: The Twentieth Century*, (London: Hamish Hamilton, 1984), p. 504.

3. Home Office, *Report of the Royal Commission on the Press 1947-1949*, (London: His Majesty's Stationery Office, June 1949), Cmd. 7700.

4. quoted in Sigal, Leon V., *Reporters and Officials*, (1973), p. 88, and in *Final Report of the [Third] Royal Commission on the Press*, Chairman: Prof. O.R. McGregor, later Lord McGregor of Durris, (London: Her Majesty's Stationery Office, July 1977), Cmnd. 6810.

5. *Articles of Constitution*, (London: The General Council of the Press, July 1953); *Articles of Constitution* [Revised], (London: The Press Council, July 1963), Article 2.

6. Rt. Hon. Lord Devlin PC; speech to the Commonwealth Press Union, London, June 1963; in *The Press and the People, 10th Annual Report of the Press Council*, (London: The Press Council, 1963), pp. 1-3.

7. *Final Report of the [Third] Royal Commission on the Press, supra* note 4.

8. "To encourage the others," as noted by Voltaire in Chapter 23 of *Candide*. Admiral John Byng was sent to relieve the garrison at the Spanish island of Minorca in 1756 but retired without doing so after an inconclusive engagement with the French. Court martialed for neglect of duty, he was found guilty, sentenced to death, and shot on his own quarter-deck in 1757.

9. General Press Release 119, Australian Press Council, Sydney, Australia, July 24, 1990.

10. *Ibid.*

Index

Abrams, Floyd, 77
Advertising Standards Authority, 133
Alton Telegraph, 68
American Arbitration Association, 36, 90, 93, 97-98, 104, 121
   Mediation and Arbitration Rules, 104
American Bar Association, 36
American Bar Association Journal, 77, 78
American Newspaper Guild, 45
American Revolution, 115
American Society of Newspaper Editors, 4, 50, 55, 67
   Canons of Journalism, 55
Annenberg Washington Program in Communications Policy Studies, The, 4, 65, 66, 119
   Libel Reform Act, 4, 69, 72, 77, 79, 80
   Proposal for the Reform of Libel Law: The Report of the Libel Reform Project, 4, 22, 65, 66, 76, 77, 78, 79, 80, 97, 119, 120, 121, 124
Aristotle, 57
Aronson, James, 11

Arthur, William, 27
Ashe, Eddie, 50
Assembly of the Republic, 135
Associated Press, 33, 52
Associated Press Managing Editors Association, 55
Association for Education in Journalism and Mass Communication, 36
Association of American Publishers, Inc., 67
Astor, Col. the Hon. J.J., 131
Australian Press Council, 136, 145
Baldwin, Stanley, 129, 130
Baltimore Sun, 51
Baron, Sandra S., 67
Bartlett, David, 5, 113
Beaverbrook, Lord, 129
Benjamin, Burton, 56
Bingham, Barry, 50
Black, Supreme Court Justice Hugo, 116, 117, 118
Bonfils, Frederick G., 55
Borzello, Bob, 137

Boston Globe, 77
Bradlee, Ben, 19, 52, 54
British Press Council, xi, xii, 3, 15, 17, 45, 50, 60, 123, 124, 127, 128, 130, 131, 132, 134, 135, 136, 137, 138, 139, 140, 141, 142, 144, 145, 146
Broadcasting Complaints Commission, 136, 139
Brown, John, 53
Brown, Lee, 56
Bull, John V. R., 53
Burnett, Carol, 68
Cabinet (British), 135
Calcutt Committee, *see* Committee on Privacy and Related Matters
Calcutt, David, QC, 127, 139
Canadian Press, 48
Carmichael, John, 45
Carroll, John S., 53
CBS, 20, 56, 68, 85, 113, 118
CBS News, 56, 59, 118, 119
  see also Westmoreland v. CBS
Chafee, Zechariah, Jr., 8
Chicago Journalism Review, 11
Chicago Sun-Times, 58
Chicago Tribune, 78
Christian Science Monitor, 77
City of London Police, 134
Cleghorn, Reese, xii, 1
College of William and Mary, Law School, 66
  Institute of Bill of Rights Law, at, 66
  William and Mary Law Review, 79
Columbia Journalism Review, 9, 11
Columbia University, 77
  Gannett Center for Media Studies, 77
  Graduate School of Journalism, 9
Commission on Freedom of the Press, 8, 9, 10, 11, 15, 17
Committee on Privacy and Related Matters, 127, 132, 138, 139, 140, 141, 143, 144, 145, 146
  Proposal of, 135, 136, 145, 146
Communications Lawyer, 76
Conselho de Inprensa, 135

Cooke, Janet, 19
Corson, Ed, 16
Cranberg, Gilbert, 77
Cunningham, Richard, 5, 6, 9, 43
Daily Star (England), 140
Dallas Morning News, 51
DeBakey, Dr. Michael, 19
Dennis, Everette, 77
Denver Post, 55
Des Moines Register, 77
Devlin, Lord, 132, 133
Duff, Philip, 33, 45
Edmonton Journal, 53
Emporia (Kan.) Gazette, 61
Encyclopaedia Britannica, 8
European Declaration of Human Rights, 128
Federal Communications Commission, 4, 23, 66, 67
Federal Rules of Evidence, 110
Fein, Bruce E., 67
Financial Times (England), 140
First Amendment, xii, xiii, 2, 3, 4, 12, 21, 33, 37, 48, 60, 66, 67, 69, 72, 73, 74, 76-77, 77, 114, 115, 116, 117, 118, 120, 121, 123, 124, 125, 128, 129
Flint, David, 145, 146
Forer, Judge Lois G., 67
Freedom of Information Act, 129
Garbus, 85
General Council of the Press, *see* British Press Council
General Medical Council, 130
General Purposes Committee, 136
Gerald, J. Edward, 23, 45, 61
Gertz v. Robert Welch, Inc., 84
Glasser, Theodore, 53
Green, Bill, 52
Guardian (England), 140
Guccione, Bob, 118
Hamilton, W. P., 130
Hartford Courant, 5, 46, 47, 59
Harvard University, 8
  Harvard Law School, 67
  Harvard Law Review, 78

Harwood, Richard, 54
Herchenroeder, John, 49, 50, 53
Hermanson, Louise, xii, 3, 15, 47
Home Secretary, 127, 128, 135
Honderich, Belend, 48
House of Commons, 139, 140
House of Lords, 134
Hubbard, Stanley, 46
Hustler Magazine, 118
Hutchins Commission, *see* Commission on Freedom of the Press
Hutchins, Robert Maynard, 8
Independent, The (England), 140
Institute of Journalists, 145
Isaacs, Norman, 19, 49, 50, 53, 56
Johnson, Fred, 25
Johnston, Harry M., III, 76
Jones, Donald (Casey), 53
Journal of College and University Law, 78
Kadet v. Daytona (Fla.) Times, 94
Kansas City Star, 47, 53, 54
Kansas City Star & Times, 19
Kansas Editorial Association, 55
Kant, Immanuel, 57
Kaplar, Richard T., xiii
Kaufman, Henry R., 76
Keker & Brochett, 79
Kent Commission, 48
Kierstead, Robert L., 77
Kipling, Rudyard, 130
Kirtley, Jane, 77
Klein, Samuel E., 67
KSTP-TV, 46
"L.A. Law," 35
Lambeth, Edmund, 57
Landers, Ann, 53
Langer, Ralph, 51
Lasswell, Harold D., 8
Lauer, Kent, 51, 53
Lemmon, John M., 51
Leval, U.S. District Judge Pierre N., 78, 86
Lewis, Anthony, 67
Lexington (Ky.) Herald-Leader, 53

Libel Defense Resource Center, 66, 76
Libel Dispute Resolution Program, *see* University of Iowa Libel Dispute Resolution Program
Libel Reform Act, *see* Annenberg Washington Program Libel Reform Act
Libel Reform Proposal, *see* Annenberg Washington Program *Proposal for the Reform of Libel Law: The Report of the Libel Reform Project*
Lord Chancellor, 128, 135
"Lou Grant," 35
Louisville Courier-Journal, 49, 54
Louisville Times, 49, 53
Luce, Henry R., 8
MacDougall, Fraser, 48
MacLeish, Archibald, 8
Macon (Ga.) Telegraph and News, Editorial Page Advisory Board and the Editorial Advisory Board of, 16
Mazer, Roslyn A., 67
McGregor, Lord of Durris, 133
McMurtry, Larry, 10
McNulty, Henry, 59
Meadows, David, 79
Media/Professional Insurance, Inc., 67
Medical Economics, 21
Mendelson, Charles, 27
Mill, John Stuart, 57, 113
Milton, Chad E., 67
Milwaukee Journal, 50
Minneapolis Star, 60
Minneapolis Star Tribune, 53
Minneapolis Tribune, 45, 50, 51, 52, 54, 60
Minnesota News Council, xi, xii, 15, 17, 18, 20, 24, 25, 32, 33, 37, 44, 45, 46, 47, 58, 60, 122, 123
Minnesota Newspaper Association, 33, 45
Minnesota Press Council, *see* Minnesota News Council
Minow, Newton N., 4, 66
Mobil Oil Corporation, 67, 68, 118
Morgan, Kenneth, xii, 3, 127

Murry, Anthony S., 67
Nashville Tennessean, 55
National Enquirer, 68
National Law Journal, 77
National News Council, xi, xii, 3, 15, 17, 18, 19, 20, 21, 22, 23, 25, 26, 28, 29, 31, 32, 37, 46, 47, 52, 57, 122, 123, 125
National Nudist Council, 25
National Public Radio, 46, 47
National Union of Journalists, 131, 145
NBC, 67
NBC News, 56, 67
Neary v. Regents of the University of California, 78, 79
New York Daily News, 19
New York Magazine, 26
New York Times, 18, 31, 46, 51, 67, 116
New York Times Co. v. Sullivan, 84, 116, 117, 118, 119, 121
New York Times Magazine, 49
New York University, 5
New York World, Bureau of Accuracy and Fair Play at, 50
Niebuhr, Reinhold, 8
Northwestern University, 19, 65
Official Secrets Act, 129
Oklahoma State University, 51
O'Neill, Michael J., 19
Ontario Press Council, 48
Organization of News Ombudsmen, 49
Owatonna (Minn.) People's Press, 33
Parade Magazine, 26
Parliament, 124, 127, 130, 135
PBS, 56
Penthouse Magazine, 118
Philadelphia Inquirer, 53, 54
Press Association (England), 140
Press Complaints Commission, xii-xiii, 3, 127, 135, 144, 145
Press Council of British Columbia, 136
Press Council, The, *see* British Press Council

Prichard, Peter S., 54
Pulitzer, Ralph, 50
Pulitzer Prize, 52, 58
Queen's Privy Council, 134
Rabbit, Jessica, 113
Radio-Television News Directors Association, 5, 55
Raskin, A. H., 49, 53
Red Wing (Minn.) Republican Eagle, 33, 45
Reluctant Reformation, The, 56
Renton, Tim, MP, 140, 141
Reporters Committee for Freedom of the Press, 77
Reuben, Don, 78
Reuter Trustees, 133
Ringhofer, Jerry, 33
Riverside Press Enterprise, 46
Rothermere, Lord, 129
Royal Commission on the Press, 130, 131, 132, 133
Sacramento Bee, 54
St. Louis Post-Dispatch, 50
St. Louis Journalism Review, 11
Salant, Richard, 56, 59
San Francisco Bay Guardian, 46
Saturday Review, 11
Schafer, Robert, 24
Schiavone Construction Company, 118
Schlesinger, Arthur M., 8
Schmertz, Herbert, 67
Schmidt, Richard M., Jr., 4, 65, 67
Schulman, Robert, 53
Schumer, Rep. Charles, 76
Seattle Times, 46
Sedition Act of 1798, 115
Seib, Charles B., 54
Severson, Thor, 54
Sharon, General Ariel, 68, 118, 119
Sharon v. Time, Inc., xi, 85, 118
Shaw, Robert, 45
Shellum, Bernie, 45
Siegal, Allan M., 51
Siegenthaler, John, 55, 56
Silha, Otto, 20

Smolla, Rodney A., 66, 78, 79, 80
Social Responsibility of the Press, 61
Society of Professional Journalists, 7, 36, 55, 56, 60
Soloski, John, 4, 83
Spielman, Gordon, 45
Stanford University, Department of Journalism, 53
State Department, 8
Stepp, Carl Sessions, 11
Stevenson, Hugh, 59
Stoppard, Tom, 131
Straus, Peter, 19
Sullivan, 116
   see also *New York Times Co. v. Sullivan*
Sulzberger, Arthur Hays, 46
Sun, The (England), 140
Tavoulareas, William, 68, 118
Tavoulareas v. Washington Post Co., xi, 67
Teapot Dome oilfield, 55
Time Magazine, 31, 68, 118, 119
Time, Inc., 8, 31, 76, 85
   see also *Sharon v. Time, Inc.*
Times, The (England), 131, 140
Traynor, Michael, 78, 79
"Tribune," see "Lou Grant"
Toronto Star, 48
Torstar, 48
Twentieth Century Fund, 17
Uniform Law Commissioners, 120, 124
   Uniform libel law proposal, 120, 121, 124
U.S. Bill of Rights, 12, 116
U.S. Congress, 2, 83, 116
U.S. Constitution, 12, 55, 115, 116, 125
U.S. Department of Justice Civil Rights Division, 67
U.S. Supreme Court, 24, 74, 75, 84, 115, 115-116, 116, 117

University of California at Berkeley, Boalt Hall School of Law, 78
   see also *Neary v. Regents of the University of California*
University of Chicago, 8
University of Iowa, 4, 66, 77
   Iowa Libel Research Project, 4, 83, 86, 87, 88, 90, 95, 98, 121, 124
   Libel Dispute Resolution Program, 4, 83, 90, 91, 94, 95, 96, 97, 98, 102, 104, 107, 121, 122, 124
University of London, 59
University of Maryland, 10
   College of Journalism, 10
University of Minnesota, 3
   School of Journalism, 45
University of Missouri, 55
University of South Alabama, 47
USA Today, 51, 55
Voltaire, 113, 143
Waller, Michael, 47
Washington Journalism Review, 9, 11
Washington Post, 19, 31, 50, 52, 54, 68, 113, 118
   see also *Tavoulareas v. Washington Post Co.*
Washington Post Writer's Group, 54
Westmoreland, Gen. William, 20, 56, 68, 118, 119
Westmoreland v. CBS, Inc., xi, 67, 78, 85, 118
WGBH-TV, 56
White, Isaac D., 50
White, William Allen, 61
William and Mary Law Review, 79
Williams, Walter, 55
Wissler, Roselle L., 4, 83
World Association of Press Councils, 145
World Court in Geneva, 31
World War II, 129, 130
Yale University, 8

The Media Institute

The Media Institute is a nonprofit, tax-exempt research foundation supported by a wide range of foundations, corporations, associations, and individuals. The Institute publishes studies analyzing media coverage of major public-policy issues, and sponsors a host of programs related to the new technologies, the First Amendment, and other communications policy issues. To support the work of the Institute, or for further information, please contact Patrick D. Maines, President, The Media Institute, 3017 M Street, N.W., Washington, D.C. 20007.

Beyond the Courtroom: Alternatives for Resolving Press Disputes was produced by David P. Taggart. Sharon Anthony provided editorial assistance and compiled the index.